A Guide to Bandelier National Monument

Third Edition

by
Dorothy Hoard

photography by
Betty Lilienthal

drawings by
the author

Los Alamos Historical Society
Los Alamos, New Mexico
1989

Cover design by Kathi Geoffrion Parker *from a photograph by* Dorothy Hoard

2nd Printing, 1994

Library of Congress Cataloging-in-Publication Data

Hoard, Dorothy.
  A guide to Bandelier National Monument / by Dorothy Hoard;
photography by Betty Lilienthal; drawings by the author.—3rd ed.
      p.   cm.
  Includes bibliographical references.
  ISBN 0-941232-09-3
  1. Hiking—New Mexico—Bandelier National Monument—Guide-books.
2. Natural history—New Mexico—Bandelier National Monument.
3. Bandelier National Monument (N.M.)—Guide-books.   I. Title.
GV199.42.N62B364   1989
917.89′56—dc20   89-27296
                                                           CIP

Originally published in 1977 by Adobe Press of Albuquerque as *A Hiker's Guide to Bandelier National Monument*

Revised edition published in 1983 by Los Alamos Historical Society as *A Guide to Bandlier National Monument*

Printed in Caledonia typeface
Printed in the United States of America

CONTENTS

I. Preface to the Third Edition v
Introduction vi
Adolph Bandelier 1
Charles F. Lummis 2
History of the Monument 3
Geology 7
Weather 9

II. Trails Originating from:
Visitor Center
Ruins Trail 13
Falls Trail 15
Frijoles Canyon 22
State Road 4
Frey Trail 29
Tyuonyi Overlook Trail 33
Burnt Mesa 38
Apache Spring Trail 42
Detached Section
Tsankawi 47
Duchess Castle 49

III. Wilderness Trails Originating from:
Visitor Center
Frijolito Trail 52
Lower Alamo Trail 54
Stone Lions Trail 60
West Alamo Rim Trail 71
Ponderosa Campground
Upper Alamo Trail 75
St. Peter's Dome
Capulin Canyon 83
Boundary Peak Trail 86
Picacho Trail 89
Eagle Canyon Pumice Mine
Cañada-Capulin Trail 92

IV. Glossary 98
Selected References 102
Index 103

SAFETY PRECAUTIONS

Carry water.

Never travel alone.

Use a topographic map when traveling cross country.

Always carry some warm clothing in wilderness areas.

Do not handle wild animals.

Carry water.

PARK SERVICE REGULATIONS

Collecting artifacts is prohibited.

Disturbing archeological or historic sites is prohibited.

Hunting or harassing wildlife is prohibited.

Pets are prohibited, except on leash in Frijoles Canyon parking lot.

Camping is prohibited in certain areas.

Motorized vehicles and equipment are prohibited in wilderness areas.

Livestock grazing is prohibited. Pack animals are allowed for day use only.

Fishing is permitted with a valid state license.

A wilderness permit is required in wilderness areas. Permits are available free at the visitor center or by calling (505) 672-3861.

PREFACE TO THE THIRD EDITION

A national monument and a wilderness—dynamic, living, evolving, growing entities. Though the mandate of the National Park Service states its purpose as "Preserving for future generations . . . ," the land, its amenities, and its visitors do change over time. This third edition documents a few of those changes since the book first appeared in 1977.

In entering its third edition, this little guide is allowed to evolve, change, and grow with our beloved park. I thank the Los Alamos Historical Society for its continuing commitment to the book, and especially for its broader purpose of presenting and interpreting our history and our times.

Eagle Canyon Pumice Mine

Sanchez Canyon

Cerro Picacho

Medio Canyon

St. Peter's Dome

Painted Cave

Kiva House

Cochiti Lake

INTRODUCTION

Bandelier National Monument is located in north-central New Mexico about five miles south of Los Alamos and an hour's drive from Santa Fe. The monument occupies the southernmost section of the Pajarito Plateau, a gently-sloping bench which skirts the eastern flank of the Jemez Moun-

tains. The entire plateau contains a wealth of archeological ruins dating from A.D. 1075 to 1550. Large pueblos, medium-sized house-blocks, single-room shelters, and cave dwellings are evidence of almost 500 years of Indian occupation. Bandelier National Monument was established to protect and preserve a part of this heritage.

The visitor complex in Frijoles

vi

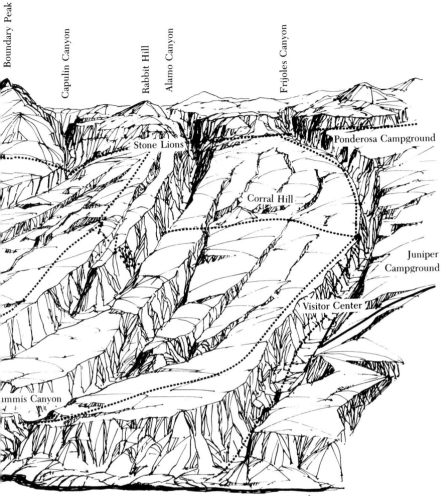

Boundary Peak

Capulin Canyon

Rabbit Hill

Alamo Canyon

Frijoles Canyon

Stone Lions

Ponderosa Campground

Corral Hill

Juniper Campground

Visitor Center

mmis Canyon

Rio Grande

Canyon is accessible by motor vehicle; Bandelier is otherwise a hiker's park. Three large canyons cross the monument, with a complex system of mesas and secondary canyons separating them. The rugged wilderness south of Frijoles Canyon is laced with a network of trails. In the main, this is high-desert country, grading from pinyon-juniper and ponderosa pine forests on the plateau to aspen-mixed conifer stands in the western mountains. Elevations range from 5,320 feet at the Rio Grande on the east to 10,199 feet at Cerro Grande on the northern border. Much of the monument has been designated a unit of the National Wilderness Preservation System, "to secure for the American people of present and future generations the benefits of an enduring resource of wilderness."

Adolph F. Bandelier (1840–1914). *Collections of the Museum of New Mexico.*

ADOLPH BANDELIER

Bandelier National Monument is named for Adolph Bandelier (1840–1914), who did pioneer research in the monument area, and whose novel, *The Delight Makers*, describes life in the prehistoric settlements of Frijoles Canyon. Bandelier (who pronounced his surname in the French manner: "ban-del-yay") is often spoken of as having been Swiss. Although he was born in Switzerland, the family emigrated to the New World when he was eight years old. (He became a naturalized U.S. citizen in 1877.) Bandelier spent his early years in Highland, Illinois, 40 miles east of St. Louis, where his father was partner in the local bank. It first appeared that the younger Bandelier, like his father, would be a businessman, but upon reaching maturity he gradually abandoned commercial ventures to pursue anthropological research. A mild interest in the cultural patterns and institutions of American Indian life became a passion after he met Lewis Henry Morgan, called by some "the Father of American Ethnology." Bandelier became possessed with the desire to investigate and prove Morgan's theories concerning affinities between Mesoamerican civilizations and the Pueblo Indian cultures of the American Southwest. To this end he spent a major part of the years 1880–89 conducting field and library research in Mexico, New Mexico and Arizona. During this period he visited the area of the present monument on at least five occasions. He also familiarized himself with the customs of contemporary Pueblo Indians by living at Cochiti and several other pueblos for extended periods.

Bandelier was an ethnologist and historian rather than an archeologist. His major scholarly contribution was the description of the past made possible by combining various disciplines—ethnology, archeology, geography, history and legend.

The Delight Makers was written primarily to make money. After Morgan's death in 1881, Bandelier encountered considerable difficulty obtaining funds for his research. In 1885 the failure of his father's bank in Highland left him the sole means of support of a wife, his father, and two nieces. The book, published in 1890, contributed little to solving his financial problems. It did succeed in fulfilling another of his avowed purposes: making information about the Pueblo Indians more accessible to the public in general by "clothing sober facts in the garb of romance." Certainly, in the opening pages Bandelier paints a superb picture of Frijoles Canyon, and throughout the book gives a convincing description of what life may have been like for the people who lived there.

Bandelier left the Southwest in 1892, but conducted further research in both Mexico and South America. In 1913 he realized a lifelong ambition to study the archives of Spain, but by then was in failing health. He died in Seville in March of the following year.

1

CHARLES F. LUMMIS

Another name closely associated with the monument is that of author and adventurer Charles Lummis (1859–1928). Lummis met Adolph Bandelier in 1888, in the midst of a New Mexico sandstorm, and later commented that he knew within the afternoon that he had met an extraordinary mind. The two continued their association long after Bandelier left the Southwest in 1892.

Lummis, the son of a Methodist minister, was born and raised in Massachusetts. He was editor of a small newspaper in Ohio when, at age twenty-six, he decided to see the West. He thereupon set out— on foot—for Los Angeles, arriving five months later. The trip instilled in Lummis an ardent love of the Southwest. He served briefly as editor of the Los Angeles Times,

edited a magazine called "Out West," was librarian for the Los Angeles Public Library, and wrote a number of books. During his life he championed many causes, including drives to save the California missions and to establish both the Southwest Museum in Los Angeles and the School of American Research at Santa Fe. He had many friends among the Indians of New Mexico and was an ardent advocate of Indian rights. Lummis possessed enormous energy and drove himself mercilessly to the point of blindness in his middle years. (He subsequently recovered his sight.) He was brash, opinionated and outspoken—quite in contrast to his reserved and scholarly friend Adolph Bandelier whom Lummis held in awe. The Rito de los Frijoles and the Pajarito Plateau held a special place in his heart. His book, *The Land of Poco Tiempo*, contains a chapter set in the monument.

Charles F. Lummis (1859–1928) in Frijoles Canyon circa 1911. *Collections of the Museum of New Mexico.*

HISTORY OF THE MONUMENT

Until recently, knowledge of the prehistoric inhabitants of the Pajarito Plateau was based on a few archeological excavations carried out early in this century. This information was supplemented by traditions of modern Pueblo Indians living in the surrounding area. The excavations done in the early 1900s may be termed "glamour archeology," since they were usually confined to the very largest ruins, a class which represents only a limited sample of the time span over which prehistoric people lived in the region.

Archeological investigations conducted since 1974 have provided considerable information about earlier occupation. Campsites of Archaic-phase hunter-gatherers dating as far back as 1750 B.C. have been discovered. Very little evidence of occupation during the Developmental Pueblo Phase (A.D. 600–1100) has been found, but a major influx of Indian farmers from the West apparently began about A.D. 1075, during the period of cultural development archeologists term the Coalition Phase. Coalition-phase dwellings were small, the largest of them rarely exceeding 15 to 20 rooms.

Archeological sites of the Classic Phase which followed (A.D. 1200 to circa A.D. 1600), to which the ruins excavated in the early 1900s belong, contain a much wider range of artifacts than those of the earlier period. Classic-phase ruins on the southern Pajarito Plateau are marked by the first appearance of glazed, as opposed to carbon-painted, pottery. Some archeologists conjecture that differences in technology, patterns of settlement and social organization south of Frijoles Canyon indicate that a different population replaced the Coalition-phase settlers in that area, though not farther to the north. The language diversity among modern Indians along the Rio Grande suggests that their ancestors had different points of origin. Locally, two widely divergent tongues are spoken. Tewa belongs to the Kiowa-Tanoan family of native languages. It is spoken by contemporary Indians of the Rio Grande Valley north of White Rock Canyon, including puebloans of San Ildefonso, Santa Clara, San Juan, Tesuque, Nambe and Pojoaque. Keres is classed as a Uto-Aztecan language. Traditions of both language groups agree that the ancestors of the Keres occupied most of the dwelling sites in the monument, while the Tewa lived north of Frijoles Canyon. Today Keres is spoken in the nearby pueblos to the south: Cochiti, Santo Domingo, and San Felipe, as well as in several pueblos west of the Rio Grande. In his book *Land of Poco Tiempo*, Charles Lummis rather fancifully outlines a series of moves through the monument area which, according to Keres tradition, the inhabitants of Frijoles Canyon and their descendants made before settling at their present home, the pueblo of Cochiti.

It would appear that by 1600 Frijoles Canyon was abandoned as a permanent home site. No mention of its existence was made by

dh

Tyuonyi ruin in Frijoles Canyon is the focal point of Bandelier National Monument.

the first Spanish expeditions (Coronado, 1540; Oñate, 1598). The eastern end of the canyon was reoccupied only briefly during the Pueblo Revolt of 1680.

The region lay unknown (or at least unrecorded) until 1740, when one Captain Andres Montoya purportedly petitioned the Spanish Crown for a grant of land between Ancho and Alamo canyons, to include the canyon of the Rito de los Frijoles. A document exists claiming that in 1780 Montoya transferred what was called the Rito de los Frijoles Grant to a son-in-law, Juan Antonio Luján. Luján descendants presumably farmed the Rito de los Frijoles Grant from that year until 1811, at which time the Spanish authorities ordered the area cleared because it had become the den of outlaws. In 1814 Antonia Rosa Luján Salas, daughter of Antonio, petitioned to be allowed to return to the grant. The Salas family thereafter lived in Frijoles Canyon for many years, or so they later claimed. All had drifted away by 1883, the year Salas heirs sold the grant to American investors. In 1893, the U.S. Court of Private Land Claims ruled that these investors' claim of title based on the supposed Rito de los Frijoles Grant was invalid. Though the several petitions concerning the grant were matters of record, no evidence that such a grant had ever been awarded by either the Spanish or Mexican governments could be produced. This judgment was upheld by the U.S. Supreme Court a few years later.

Adolph Bandelier briefly visited Frijoles Canyon and other sections of the present monument area on several occasions in the

4

1880s. In the 1890s, archeologist Edgar Lee Hewett proposed that a "Pajarito National Park," encompassing the entire Pajarito Plateau, be established. Local opposition from homesteaders, ranchers, lumbermen and the Santa Clara Indians doomed that proposal. In 1905 the area became part of the newly established Jemez National Forest. Between 1908 and 1912 Hewett directed the excavation of major sites in Frijoles Canyon.

Although Frijoles Canyon was specifically excluded from homesteading because of the archeological values it contained, Judge Judson Abbott of Santa Fe, then in his seventies, settled there in 1910. Under a lease from the Forest Service, he established a resort he called "Ranch of the Ten Elders," a name inspired by the box-elder trees growing beside the stream. Abbott sold his lease in 1919. It passed through two successive ownerships before transfer to George and Evelyn Frey in 1925.

Bandelier National Monument, under the jurisdiction of the U.S. Forest Service, was established by presidential proclamation in 1916; administration was transferred to the National Park Service in 1932. The Freys remained to operate Frijoles Canyon Lodge. Evelyn Frey died in 1988 after 63 years' residence in Frijoles Canyon.

The major work of stabilizing the ruins and constructing visitor facilities was carried out between 1934 and 1937 as Civilian Conservation Corps (CCC) projects. In 1935 Evelyn Frey rode in the first

Adolph Bandelier and Adelaido Montoya of Cochiti Pueblo at cave ruins in Frijoles Canyon, December 5, 1880. Photo by George C. Bennett. *Collections of the Museum of New Mexico.*

5

automobile driven into the canyon on the newly completed road. During World War II the lodge was appropriated by the U.S. Army in connection with the Manhattan (Atomic Bomb) Project at nearby Los Alamos. Lodge operation was returned to Mrs. Frey in 1946.

Since 1950 visitor use has increased steadily. The lodge has been converted to administrative offices. The influx of visitors has forced modification of other facilities and the tightening of regulations. To insure that parts of the monument remain in natural condition, roadless sections were incorporated into the National Wilderness Preservation System in 1976.

bl

The Visitor Center in Frijoles Canyon is part of the 1934/37 CCC Project of the Great Depression.

Cliffs of Frijoles Canyon illustrate ash flow deposition of tuff formations. Long House Ruins and orchard in middle distance. About 1917. *Collections of the Museum of New Mexico.*

GEOLOGY

The present topography of Bandelier National Monument is largely the result of past volcanic activity. Most of the area is covered with thick layers of compacted volcanic ash collectively called Bandelier Tuff. (*Tuff* should not be confused with *tufa*. The latter is rock formed as mineral deposits by lakes or springs.) Underlying the tuff at the eastern margin of the monument are dark basalts laid down before the beginning of the ash eruptions.

Volcanic ash is comparatively light debris that emerges in solid rather than molten condition. Turbulent mixtures of gases and ash pour from vents of the volcano and rapidly spread in sheets over the surrounding area. The Pajarito Plateau was formed by repeated ash flows of this type. Variations of hardness of the tuff are due to the degree to which particles were welded to one another and by reactions of ash particles with gases escaping from the cooling ash flows. As the ash deposits cooled, shrinkage caused the columnar cracks visible in the cliff faces. Weathering of the harder layers has given rise to the spectacular vertical cliffs and columnar structures of the plateau.

Volcanism in the monument area occurred in connection with the formation of the Rio Grande Rift. That giant trough in the earth's crust can now be traced between Leadville, Colorado, and the state of Chihuahua in northern Mexico. As rifting progressed, a series of basins aligned *en echelon* sank at

7

White Rock Canyon of the Rio Grande is cut through basaltic and andesite flows from bl the Cerros del Rio volcanic field east of the monument. The canyon received its name from a small white deposit upstream.

different rates; the resulting strain caused the development of very deep fissures at their common boundaries. Such fissures provided pathways for a rise of magma to the surface. From the Cerros del Rio, a group of vents at the junction of the Española and Santo Domingo basins, and from vents now buried under part of the Jemez volcanic field, eruptions of basaltic lava began about three million years ago. The resulting dark rocks lie at the eastern margin of the monument.

Northwest of the Cerros del Rio, the rift intersects a preexisting zone of crustal weakness called the Jemez lineament. There, over a long period beginning about 13 million years ago, viscous lava slowly built up an extensive volcanic pile now called the Jemez Mountains. About 1.4 million years ago and again about 1.1. million years ago two series of violent eruptions spewed vast quantities of volcanic ash from magma chambers beneath the center of the pile. The resulting ash flows produced the thick layers of tuff that constitute the Pajarito Plateau.

As ash was expelled from the volcano, the structure collapsed, forming a large depression called a caldera. This was partially filled with ash deposits, then with water, but centuries of erosion choked the lake with sediments. A series of meadows now occupies a portion of the caldera. The largest of these, the Valle Grande, can be seen from State Road 4 eleven miles west of the monument.

WEATHER

Weather in the high desert is unpredictable. Only broad generalities are noted here.

Spring is usually unpleasant. From March into May, cold, strong winds are the rule. Brief but violent snowstorms can occur in March and April. Until mid-May, nighttime temperatures can fall below freezing. Late May and early June are usually pleasant and dry.

Late June and early July are the hottest times of the year; temperatures may climb to the 90s. In mid-July the thunderstorm season begins. Mornings are sunny and pleasant, but clouds begin to appear by mid-morning and by early afternoon have become towering thunderheads. Violent showers, though usually brief and localized, occur throughout the afternoon. This weather pattern continues through August and into September. Nights are cool and generally clear.

Fall weather is glorious, with clear, sparkling days. Fall colors—yellow rabbit brush and purple asters in September, golden aspen and cottonwood in October—seem even brighter under the radiant blue skies. Daytime temperatures may be in the 70s but can fall to freezing at night. Rain is usually rare and of short duration. This type of weather can persist into November.

Winters are comparatively mild, though diurnal temperature variations can be extreme. Daytime temperatures may reach the 50s while nighttime temperatures fall into the teens. January is the coldest month; temperatures can fall below 0° F. Winter snowfall is variable and unpredictable. At lower elevations in the monument snow will generally melt and disappear within a few days, though in shaded areas snow cover can persist all winter. On the trails of north-facing canyon walls packed snow can be hazardous. On occasion, the Pajarito Plateau is subject to heavy and long-lasting snowfalls. These often occur at night and would be dangerous for an unprepared backpacker.

Northern New Mexico is subject to violent electrical storms. Several people are killed each year by lightning. Hikers should be aware of safety precautions during lightning storms; do not stand under a tall tree, do not stand in an open area, do not sit in a cave (lightning tends to strike across the opening). Crouch in a depression, keeping arms and legs close to the body, until the storm passes. Hypothermia—loss of body heat—is a constant danger. Days can be very warm but the temperature falls rapidly at dark. Always carry warm clothing. Prevention is by far the best treatment for hypothermia. If a companion does become excessively chilled, warm the person as quickly as possible with warm clothing, hot fluids, even the body warmth of others.

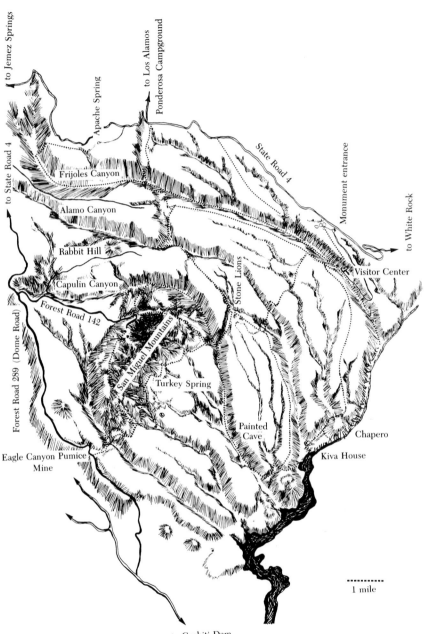

to Jemez Springs

Apache Spring

to Los Alamos

Ponderosa Campground

to State Road 4

State Road 4

Monument entrance

to White Rock

Frijoles Canyon

Alamo Canyon

Rabbit Hill

Capulin Canyon

Forest Road 142

Stone Lions

Visitor Center

Forest Road 289 (Dome Road)

San Miguel Mountains

Turkey Spring

Painted Cave

Chapero

Eagle Canyon Pumice Mine

Kiva House

1 mile

to Cochiti Dam

A Guide to
Bandelier
National Monument

bl

Frijoles Canyon is cut through ashflow deposits on the eastern flank of the Jemez Mountains. Pajarito Mountain (10,441 ft) at top, right.

Trailheads at the
VISITOR CENTER

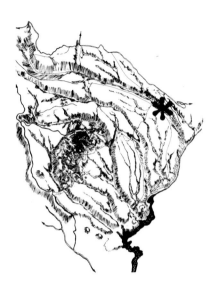

Monument headquarters in Frijoles Canyon is the focal point of Bandelier. A paved road leads to the Visitor Center where parking is available. Three easy and popular trails originate here. Every visitor to the monument should walk the paved Ruins Trail through Tyuonyi and the cliff dwellings. The Falls Trail and Frijoles Canyon Trail offer moderate hiking through the well-watered, well-wooded canyon.

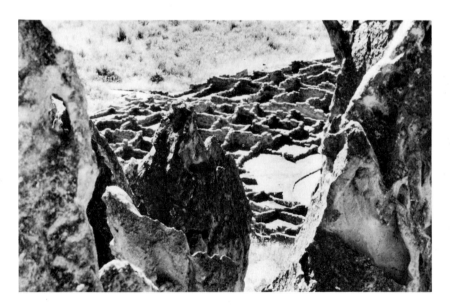

Tyuonyi. Photo by Leroy N. Sanchez.

An extensive series of cave dwellings line the north wall of Frijoles Canyon. Reconstructed cliff house is at left, center. Walls of Tyuonyi in foreground.

RUINS TRAIL

An impressive and beautiful archeological area is located within easy walking distance of the Visitor Center in Frijoles Canyon. The ruins of the pueblo of Tyuonyi, estimated to have been three stories high, are located here. *Tyuonyi* is a Keres word. Adolph Bandelier claimed that it means "place of treaty," and refers to some remote pact between Keres and Tewa Indians defining their boundaries. Later linguists could not verify this definition, but archeologists agree that Frijoles Canyon seems to have been the border between Keres and Tewa territory. The Tewa called the ruin *Puqwige'onwikeji*, "old pueblo where the bottoms of the pottery vessels were smoothed thin."

The site was excavated by Edgar Hewett and his School of American Archeology (now the School of American Research) from 1908 to 1911. Additional work was done in 1933 and in 1937/38 by the CCC. Adjacent to Tyuonyi is a large, fully excavated kiva, or ceremonial chamber. Beyond Tyuonyi the trail leads past two extensive series of cliff dwellings which lie at the base of the south-facing cliff. The convolutions of the path among the tent rocks and the rugged ladders leading to several of the caves make this trail a favorite with children.

The Park Service provides a pamphlet describing points of interest along the Ruins Trail. Guided tours are available in season. On nature trails beside the stream, informative plaques identify canyon plants, birds and mammals.

Charles Lummis at cliff dwellings in Frijoles Canyon. Lummis insisted on sleeping in caves when visiting the canyon. Circa 1916. *Collections of the Museum of New Mexico.*

FALLS TRAIL

In addition to being a beautiful and moderate walk, the Falls Trail down the canyon of the Rito de los Frijoles provides a journey through the geologic history of the monument. Three million years of geologic time are represented as the path descends through layers of Bandelier Tuff and the underlying Cerros del Rio volcanic rocks to sedimentary layers that fill the Rio Grande Rift.

Falls Trail is well maintained, though stream crossings vary in difficulty. The canyon is subject to flooding, and Park Service bridges periodically are destroyed. The trail begins at the eastern edge of the Visitor Center parking lot. Initially it traverses a barren and exposed slope before descending to stream level. Black cliffs on the

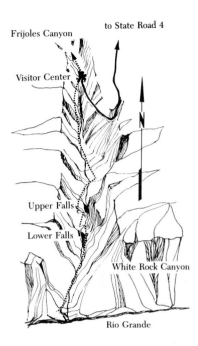

FALLS TRAIL

Visitor Center to:

Upper Falls	1.3 mi	2.1 km
Lower Falls	1.5	2.4
Rio Grande	2.4	3.9

opposite side of the stream mark the top of Cerros del Rio lava flows, laid down before ash erupted from the Jemez volcano.

Scattered along the canyon floor, most noticeably in a clump about a half-mile beyond the trailhead, are teepee-shaped tuff formations. Unlike tentrocks protected by a caprock, these were formed by a special mechanism. They are the remnants of fumeroles, escape paths for hot gases. Here the ash was far from its source and no longer retained sufficient heat to weld the particles. But where the ash flowed over small bodies of water, steam flashed upward,

dh

Fumarole tentrocks. Note the swirl patterns of gas bubbles along the sides.

causing chemical reactions that hardened the rock. Over time, softer surrounding tuff eroded away, exposing these more resistant cones. The spiral markings along the skirts identify escape paths of swirling hot gases. Fumarole tentrocks are fairly common in Bandelier.

A mile beyond the trailhead the canyon broadens into a level wooded area. The north wall is a fine cliff of orange tuff sandwiched between sections of black basalt. The tuff formation represents the cross section of an ancient canyon filled by the ash flows. This is one piece of evidence indicating that canyons existed on the Pajarito Plateau before the ash eruptions and are being recarved through tuff deposits.

Note the charming cluster of tentrocks at the east end of the canyon, flanked on the south by a dark wall that abruptly narrows the canyon. The trail climbs the steep south slope. Until the trail was carved out of the rock, lower Frijoles Canyon was quite inaccessible. Adolph Bandelier commented in his journal that the valley is almost fully closed on the east, where it enters the Rio Grande which flows through a fearful dark canyon. The Rito rushes through a narrow cleft and cascades down a black basalt cliff. These Upper Falls are best seen from a vantage point halfway down the slope as the trail descends to stream level.

The geology of the lower canyon is strikingly different. The orange tuff is gone. The dark canyon walls show striped patterns, remnants of a buried maar volcano. Maars form when water flows into a volcanic vent. Heat from the lava produces a steam explosion; the escaping steam carries volcanic

Upper Falls of the Rito de los Frijoles.

d h

16

bl

Colorful striped maar deposits underlie dark andesitic cliffs on the northeast wall of Frijoles Canyon.

debris with it. The debris settles around the vent to form a low cone of layered material. This example in Frijoles Canyon is but one of a series of maar craters that extends across the Cerros del Rio volcanic field. The craters mark the course of the ancestral Rio Grande.

A thin layer of red stone is prominent on the eastern wall of Frijoles Canyon. It is a tuff deposit from a maar volcano. When hot lava later flowed over it, iron compounds in the tuff oxidized to bright red. The dark cliff above the red band is andesite, which forms a thicker and more pasty lava than does basalt. The contorted, tortured features of the cliff face form when layers of the lava flow are still moving as the mass of the rock cools. This cliff is also part of the sequence of Cerros del Rio flows.

Through the portal of Frijoles Canyon is visible White Rock Canyon of the Rio Grande, which marks the eastern edge of the Jemez ash flows.

The vegetation along the Falls Trail differs from that of the surrounding countryside. In contrast to the sparse pigmy evergreen forest of the mesas, the canyon is lined with tall deciduous trees. Narrowleaf cottonwoods predominate. The name refers to hairs that cover the seeds. On a windy day in late spring this "cotton" fills the air and covers the ground like blowing snow. Cottonwoods are dioecious with male and female flowers on different trees. (Municipalities that plant cottonwoods for shade avoid cotton litter by planting only male trees.) Narrowleaf cottonwood has willow-like leaves and light-col-

17

Female flowers of the box elder droop from the branches in early spring.

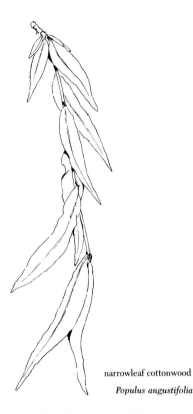

narrowleaf cottonwood
Populus angustifolia

ored, deeply furrowed bark.

Also common along the rito is box elder, a species of maple. It has the typical winged seeds of the family, but the three-parted compound leaves are distinctive. Box-elders have been "boxed," or tapped, for their sap, though the syrup is much inferior to that of sugar maples. This tree is also dioecious. In spring watch for delicate, petalless flowers on long slender stems hanging from the branches.

Dioecism is not prevalent in the plant world; only about sixty families of the four hundred world-wide have any dioecious members. An advantage to desert plants is that the pollen is windblown and does not depend upon insects or other animals for dispersal. Also, cross-pollination, which produces sturdier offspring, is assured.

Interspersed among the cotton-woods and box elders are tree-sized Gambel oaks. They have bright green, deeply lobed leaves. Elsewhere on the Pajarito Plateau, Gambel oak is more commonly found scattered in low thickets atop the mesas. Prehistoric Indians utilized acorns as a food source, grinding them into a flour, but had to leach out bitter tannins with water before the flour could be eaten. They preferred the acorns of Gambel oak, which are less bitter than the acorns of other species. Oaks are still the principal source of the tannins used to tan leather. Until very recently tannins were also used in medicine to treat burns. Indians used a tea brewed from oak bark to treat sore throat, mouth inflammation or toothache.

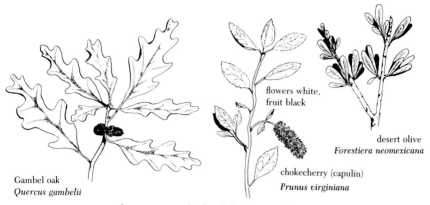

flowers white,
fruit black

desert olive
Forestiera neomexicana

chokecherry (capulin)
Prunus virginiana

Gambel oak
Quercus gambelii

Three common shrubs of the Pajarito Plateau.

A common shrub in these lower canyons of the Pajarito Plateau is desert, or New Mexico, olive. It, too, is a dioecious species with male and female flowers on separate plants. In early spring the flowers bloom before the leaves come out, giving the branches a yellowish cast. The bitter fruit resembles a small olive.

Capulin, also called choke-cherry, likewise occurs along the Falls Trail. This shrub or small tree grows from six to eight feet tall. The bright green leaves are very finely toothed at the margins. In spring, small white flowers bloom in bunches at the ends of the branches and are noticeable at a considerable distance. Black berries are produced in the fall. The raw fruit is astringent and puckery but makes good syrup or jam.

On the dry slopes above Upper Falls grow two shrubs renowned in Western folklore. One, apparently leafless and with jointed stems, is joint-fir or Mormon tea. The species is dioecious; the seeds are borne on female plants in tiny cones in the angles of the branches.

Mormon tea belongs to the genus *Ephedra*, part of a group of primitive flowering plants related to the conifers. The ephedras contain ephedrine, once used in nose drops. Synthetic compounds have replaced the natural substance in most commercial preparations. Indians ate the seeds and brewed cough medicine from the branches. The tea may be effective for cough, but it tastes terrible.

Mormon tea
Ephedra viridis

19

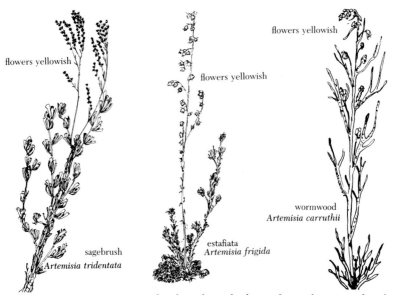

flowers yellowish

flowers yellowish

flowers yellowish

sagebrush
Artemisia tridentata

estafiata
Artemisia frigida

wormwood
Artemisia carruthii

Three common Artemisias. Sagebrush is a large shrub. Estafiata and wormwood are low plants. All have aromatic foliage.

Big Sagebrush is a shrub of similar size but bears small gray-green leaves. Each leaf ends in three rounded teeth. This is the fabled purple sage of the Golden West, and grows throughout the arid western United States. Sagebrush belongs to the sunflower family and is not related to the sage used as seasoning, which is a member of the mint family. Indians and later, Spanish settlers used sagebrush medicinally. Sagebrush tea is still held to be an infallible, though heroic, cure for the common cold. (I tried it once; the cold was preferable.)

Several sages, all members of the genus *Artemisia*, grow on the Pajarito Plateau. All have tiny flowers held in crowded clusters on long stems. The leaves have a strong, pungent odor when crushed and usually are a silvery color. Look for silver-green mounds of fringed sage, or estafiata, and for Carruth's wormwood. Both are abundant beside the Falls Trail.

The trail continues down the canyon, passing Lower Falls. Ultimately it reaches the Rio Grande in White Rock Canyon. Lower sections of the trail become rough and rocky. It is necessary to cross the rito several times on irregularly placed boulders.

The mouth of the Rito de los Frijoles lies on the flood plain of Cochiti Lake. Fluctuations in the lake level have killed the trees along the shore. The settling waters deposited inches of new soil, and annual weeds sprout in profusion amid the skeletal trees.

Due to wide fluctuations in lake level, the Park Service no longer maintains the trail that once ran beside the river downstream to the mouth of Alamo Canyon.

b1

Just above Upper Falls, lower Frijoles Canyon shelters a gentle world of pines and tent rocks.

21

FRIJOLES CANYON

Visitor Center to:

Ceremonial Cave	1	mi	1.6 km	paved
Upper Crossing	5.6		9	
Ponderosa Campground	7.3		12.2	400-ft steep ascent

The trail from the Visitor Center up Frijoles Canyon to Upper Crossing is fairly level along its six-mile length, crossing the stream many times on rocks or small logs. At Upper Crossing, trails lead south out of the canyon into the Bandelier Wilderness and north to Ponderosa Campground 1.7 miles away. Both require a strenuous 400-foot climb. Hikers often take this route from Ponderosa Campground to the Visitor Center—all downhill—leaving a car at their destination. In winter the canyon floor is usually covered with snow.

Rodents scamper and scold among the conifers. The Abert's squirrel, *Sciurus aberti*, is a handsome gray animal with long flowing tail and tasseled ears. It feeds on the ground but climbs a tree when frightened and crouches motionless among the branches. Its gray color blends with the bark and its ears resemble broken twigs. Chipmunks and golden-mantled ground squirrels, both favorites of National Park visitors throughout the West, occasionally cross the path or run along logs. Even more common is the rock squirrel, *Spermophilus variegatus*, "variegated seed-lover," the largest ground squirrel in this area. Rock squirrels were used as food by the prehistoric Indians; their bones are found in all the middens. The rock squirrel is mottled gray and has a bushy tail. The much smaller golden-mantled ground squirrel, *S. lateralis*, is coppery in color and has a white stripe bordered in black along each side. The least chipmunk, *Eutamias minimus*, "smallest good steward," resembles the golden-mantled ground squirrel but is smaller, about nine inches long, and has a dark stripe through the eye. It runs with its tail held erect.

About a mile west of the visitor center is Ceremonial Cave. It lies 150 feet above the canyon floor, but is accessible by a series of lad-

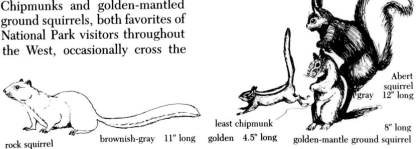

rock squirrel   brownish-gray   11″ long   least chipmunk   golden   4.5″ long   golden-mantle ground squirrel   8″ long   Abert squirrel   gray   12″ long

Some common rodents of the Pajarito Plateau.

ders. Near the front of the cave is a small kiva, or ceremonial chamber, for which the cave undoubtedly was named. The site was excavated and restored in 1910 as part of the Hewett studies. Further restoration work was carried out in the early 1940s. Along the back wall are the foundations of a number of rooms and several pens in which turkeys were kept. Hendron (1946) suggests that the name "Ceremonial Cave" is not an accurate description of its use and that the cave was merely a protected habitation site. The association of a kiva with a small group of houses was common practice. Judging from the composition of the middens, ordinary day-to-day activities were the rule. From pottery shards, Ceremonial Cave appears to have been occupied from approximately A.D. 1250 to 1600.

About a half-mile upstream from Ceremonial Cave the canyon narrows abruptly. Vertical walls of tuff rise 100 feet high and in places lie only 25 feet apart. From within, this appears to be the full extent of the canyon, but the true dimensions are much greater—half a mile wide and 500 feet deep.

A sparkling stream, fine stands of tall trees, a profusion of shrubs and small plants, animals and birds make Frijoles Canyon a delightful hike. Watch for the dipper or water ouzel, a charming gray bird about the size of a sparrow. Look for the

Judge Abbott leads a party of visitors to Ceremonial Cave. Photo by George L. Beam. *National Park Service, Bandelier National Monument.*

bl

Orange tuff cliffs close upon the streambed in Frijoles Canyon.

dipper
gray
5.75" long

white flash of its blinking eye and for the dipping curtsy it performs. The dipper flies directly into the stream and runs along the bottom, feeding on aquatic insects.

Of the welter of plants in the canyon, the hiker should avoid two. One, poison ivy, is low-growing, with bright green leaflets in sets of three. ("Leaflets three—let it be.") The plant usually grows in small patches and has pale, waxy berries. All parts of the plant contain a heavy oil that can cause skin inflammation, swelling and blisters. The reaction is allergic; that is, the first contact produces no symptoms, but sensitizes the victim so that, after a few days, subsequent contacts produce severe rashes, often requiring medical treatment. The irritant adheres to clothing and even to the fur of pets, so that it is possible to develop symptoms without touching the plant itself. Sleeping bags often become contaminated. Strong soap and hot water are necessary to remove the oily irritant.

The other plant that is a source of discomfort is the stinging nettle. Nettles grow in large patches in shady, well watered places. The plants can grow six feet in height. Fine, stiff "hairs" on the leaves cause welts that can last for hours. The hairs are hollow and act as hypodermic needles. The fluid injected is stored in a sac at the base of each hair, and contains formic acid, a chemical also found in ants. A popular first aid for nettle stings is a poultice made of mud, which soothes the pain and draws out the hairs as it dries. Nettles are edible when cooked, though they tend to be bland. Young shoots can be boiled and eaten like spinach. The leaves can be dried for tea. The plant is high in vitamin C.

Other entirely harmless plants growing along the trail are worth noting. The horsetail, or scouring rush, is a living fossil, survivor of a group of primitive plants dominant during the PaleozoicEra three

stinging nettle
Urtica gracilis

berries
pale yellow

poison ivy
Rhus radicans

hundred million years ago. The remains of tree-sized relatives of the horsetail, members of the *Equisetaceae*, make up a large part of the world's coal deposits. The name "scouring rush" was given the plant by early western miners who used it to clean pots and pans. The stems contain large amounts of silica and are quite abrasive.

Meadow rue, abundant in the canyons of the Pajarito Plateau, resembles a fern in appearance. It is, however, a true flowering plant, blooming in spring on erect stems which extend above the leaves. The most common meadow rue *Thalictrum fendleri*, is dioecious. The odd, nodding little flowers have no petals. The male flowers bear long, drooping stamens like tiny tassels.

flowers greenish, without petals

meadowrue
Thalictrum fendleri

horsetail
Equisetum arvense

flowers pink to white

valerian
Valeriana capitata

The canyon vegetation becomes more verdant near Upper Crossing, the junction of the Frijoles Canyon and Upper Alamo trails. In early spring look for the valerians, small plants about ten inches high, with tight clusters of pink flowers atop long stems. Later, look for the pretty little western red columbine with nodding red and yellow flowers.

From Upper Crossing to Ponderosa Campground on State Road 4 is 1.7 miles. The initial 400-foot climb out of Frijoles Canyon is fairly steep. The last mile is a pleasant, level hike on a fire road through the forest.

Fallen leaves carpet the path along the Rito de los Frijoles. The canyon is usually snow-covered in winter and often icy in early spring.

Trails originating along
STATE ROAD 4

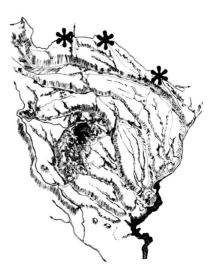

Five trails originate at various points along State Road 4. Two of these, the Frey Trail and the Tyuonyi Overlook Trail, start at Juniper Campground just inside the monument entrance. 5.65 miles west of the entrance station (left on State Road 4) is Ponderosa Campground, trailhead for access to Upper Crossing in Frijoles Canyon and the wilderness at the western edge of the monument. In addition, two fire roads branch from State Road 4. They are difficult to find but well worth the search. Burnt Mesa Fire Road lies 3.9 miles west of the monument entrance. Fire Road 3 is 1.7 miles west of Ponderosa Campground.

b1

Small, scattered mounds of brick-shaped tuff blocks mark innumerable archeological sites of the Pajarito Plateau.

FREY TRAIL

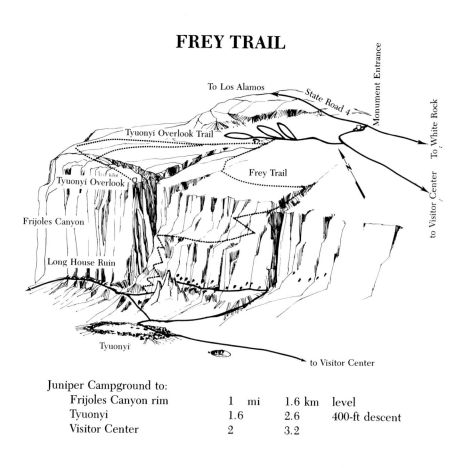

To Los Alamos

State Road 4

Monument Entrance

To White Rock

Tyuonyi Overlook Trail

Frey Trail

Tyuonyi Overlook

Frijoles Canyon

to Visitor Center

Long House Ruin

Tyuonyi

to Visitor Center

Juniper Campground to:			
Frijoles Canyon rim	1 mi	1.6 km	level
Tyuonyi	1.6	2.6	400-ft descent
Visitor Center	2	3.2	

The Frey Trail, once called the Old North Trail, was for many years the main access to Frijoles Canyon from the north rim. It was built by the Forest Service while Judge Abbott lived in the canyon. All equipment and supplies for the resorts, trees for the orchards, even an upright piano, were brought in over this trail. In 1926, George Frey, a practical engineer, built an aerial tramway for hauling supplies to the canyon floor. Visitors still entered via the trail until 1935 when the CCC completed the present road.

The trail begins near the amphitheater parking lot at Juniper Campground, and traverses the mesa a gentle mile before reaching the canyon rim. The vegetation is pinyon-juniper-grama grass association. This zone occurs throughout the Southwest at elevations between 5,000 and 7,500 feet, though species vary with locality. The pinyon of this area, *Pinus edulis*, occurs in pure stands or intermingled with juniper in pigmy forests which often cover hundreds of acres. The pinyon is the state tree of New Mexico. Its

29

seeds are indeed edible and were a staple food in the diet of the ancient inhabitants. Seed hulls are found in all the middens of the ruins. Pinyon "nuts" are still gathered outside the monument boundaries by local people in the autumn. Both pinyons and junipers are slow-growing trees. Specimens often live three hundred years or more. A pinyon will not produce nuts until it is at least seventy-five years old.

The needles of pinyon, a true pine, are about 1.5 inches long and occur in bundles of two. (Needles at the ends of branches may appear single.) The stout, top-shaped cones have large cavities containing the nuts. Both cones and bark are very pitchy. Pinyon is a favorite firewood in the Southwest, known for its fragrant, even-burning characteristics. Its use by a populace that perceives it as a cheap fuel is increasing alarmingly.

One-seed juniper occurs in association with pinyon at lower elevations and in pure stands on hot, dry sites. The species is dioecious, with male and female flowers on different trees. Female trees produce dark blue berry-like fruit, each containing a single seed. The berries are edible but bitter and astringent until after a frost. Indian children ate the berries as candy. The male trees have small, pollen-bearing cones at the ends of the branches. In spring the pollen, a common cause of hay fever, rises in great brown clouds when the branches are disturbed.

Junipers have scale-like leaves that lie flat against the branches. With one-seed juniper, branching

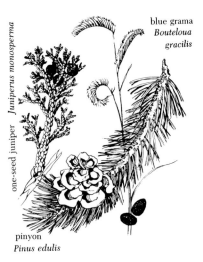

one-seed juniper *Juniperus monosperma*

blue grama *Bouteloua gracilis*

pinyon *Pinus edulis*

begins at ground level so that the plant seems more a shrub than a tree. The bark of the thick trunk peels off in long strips. Most junipers have a number of dead branches. Indians used junipers for many practical purposes. They wove the shreddy bark into sandals, blankets, baby diapers and menstrual pads. The pitch was used as a glue and as a sealant to waterproof baskets. All parts of the tree were used for medicinal purposes, especially for treating disorders of the urinary tract.

Throughout the United States junipers are often called cedars. (Botanists reserve the name for members of the Old World genus *Cedrus*.) "Cedar" fence posts are actually juniper. The wood contains oils and resins which act as preservatives and render it rot-resistant.

Blue grama, the most common grass of the mesas, grows in bunches to a height of about 18 inches. Seedheads are borne on one side of the stem, giving them the appearance of little combs. In

bl

The Frey Trail descends in switchbacks toward Tyuonyi.

winter the dry heads assume a characteristic sickle shape. Indians tied several stalks together to make delicate brushes for sweeping their metates. Other grama grasses occur in the monument, but blue grama is by far the most common.

The Frey Trail crosses the level mesa for about a mile, skirting small dry washes and traversing dusty pumice slopes. Then it dips into a side canyon before opening out onto the sheer wall above Frijoles Canyon. A fine Park Service trail descends the face of the cliff. Prior to 1935, when the present road into the canyon was completed, all visitors entered by this trail. It was a spectacular sight in contrast to the monotonous mesas: a peaceful valley, cultivated fields and an orchard. Cottonwoods lined the little stream whose murmur was audible even 500 feet up the canyon wall. Upstream, pine groves crowded the canyon floor, downstream, a dark cliff of black rock closed the canyon like a sack, with only a narrow opening showing the dark walls of White Rock Canyon beyond. In the center directly below was the perfect circle marking the ancient pueblo of Tyuonyi.

Today, the view is much the same. The fields have reverted to native plants and the orchard is untended. Pueblo-style, flat-roofed Park Service buildings huddle in harmony with the cottonwoods and the orange cliffs.

Along the cliff face during the summer the canyon wren sings its unmistakable song, a liquid cas-

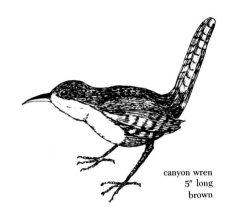

canyon wren
5″ long
brown

cade of descending notes. Fortunate hikers may occasionally see the charming little bird hopping on boulders beside the trail. It is brown with a long erect reddish tail, long black bill, and white breast.

In places the trail is cut into solid tuff. The various textures of the tuff are due to the effects of gases released as the ash flows cooled. Note that there is no definite line between adjacent layers. The flows followed one another in rapid succession—within hours or a few days. The entire mass then lost heat slowly, sometimes taking as long as ten years to cool. The resulting formation is called a *cooling unit*.

Near the floor of the canyon the Frey Trail switches down a dry and dusty pumice slope that represents volcanic ash fall deposits. Then it joins the paved Ruins Trail near Tyuonyi, about a half mile from the Visitor Center.

TYUONYI OVERLOOK TRAIL

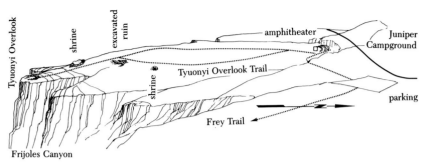

Tyuonyi Overlook · shrine · excavated ruin · amphitheater · Juniper Campground · Tyuonyi Overlook Trail · shrine · parking · Frey Trail

Frijoles Canyon

Amphitheater to:
Tyuonyi Overlook
loop

	1.2 mi	3.1 km	level
	2	3.2	

Starting near the amphitheater at Juniper Campground, the Tyuonyi Overlook Trail describes a loop on the level mesa. A short extension follows a finger-like spur to a viewpoint overlooking Tyuonyi and the Visitor Center in Frijoles Canyon. Overall the trail is good, though it becomes somewhat rocky as it nears the canyon rim. With a round-trip distance of only two miles, it is an ideal early morning or evening hike. The Park Service has installed signs illustrating features of the mesa and its vegetation. A small ruin and two shrines lie along the route.

The trail traverses the intersection of two plant communities; ponderosa pines intermingle with pinyons and junipers. Ponderosa pine, also called western yellow pine, is the second most important source of lumber in the United States, exceeded only by Douglas fir. The trees can grow 120 feet tall. They bear long needles in bundles of three. Large trees have cinnamon-colored bark with a distinct vanilla-like odor. Smaller trees have dark bark and are called "black jack" pines. Pine seeds have strict germination requirements and seedlings survive only in a few favorable years, consequently the trees in a single stand of ponderosa pine, large and small alike, are likely to be of the same age. Indians used ponderosa logs as roof beams, burning them to size by placing hot coals against the trunks.

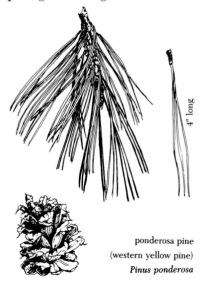

4" long

ponderosa pine
(western yellow pine)
Pinus ponderosa

33

Spanish bayonet, datil (yucca) *Yucca baccata*

Indians made extensive use of other plants common on the mesas. Look for the yucca plant, the Indians' supermarket. From the leaves came fibers for cord and rope from which were fashioned fishing nets, bowstrings, sandals and baskets. Most parts of the plant were eaten, though some required extensive preparation such as roasting or drying. Yuccas also had medicinal properties, especially for arthritis, a common affliction of prehistoric Indians. Yucca needles were used as paintbrushes to scribe designs on pottery. Rubbing yucca roots into a lather with water provided a good shampoo and soap for both Indians and European settlers even into modern times. Yucca, the state flower of New Mexico, is a member of the lily family. It blooms in spring with large, showy, cream-colored flowers. Two species grow on the Pajarito Plateau: the narrowleaf yucca and the Spanish bayonet or datil, with wide, stout leaves. The latter was the more useful to the Indians. Yuccas illustrate an extreme type of biological interdependence. They require a certain species of small moth, *Pronuba*, to pollinate their flowers. The moth, in turn, cannot reproduce on any other plant.

Look, too, for mountain mahogany, a tall shrub with small oval leaves. The Indians used its heavy wood for looms and utensils. The botanical name *Cercocarpus montanus*, literally "mountain tailed-fruit," refers to the seeds, which have long, feathery, spiraled tails. These straighten when moistened, then recurl upon drying,

flower (25x)

mountain mahogany
Cercocarpus montanus

an action which tends to drill the seeds into the ground after a rain. The flowers of the mountain mahogany are small, inconspicuous and green. The stamens are arranged around the rim of a little cup, a characteristic of the rose family to which the plant belongs. Mountain mahogany is unrelated to true mahogany which is found in the tropics.

Other plants of the mesa are neither romantic nor utilitarian; some are indicators of overgrazing. Snakeweed, a small, bright green shrub about 18 inches high, blooms in August with a mass of yellow flowers. Broom groundsel is similar in appearance. Both thrive on overgrazed ranges. False tarragon, a weedy shrub with narrow leaves and reddish-brown stems, is another sign of overgrazing. This plant is said to grow where sheep once grazed. (In the latter half of the nineteenth century New Mexico was the largest sheep-producing area in the country, and the Pajarito Plateau saw its share of sheep grazing.) Cholla and prickly pear cactus are also invaders of disturbed land.

The excavated ruin at the junction with the return trail is typical of the hundreds of small-house dwellings once scattered over the Pajarito Plateau. The majority of them were located in the pinyon-juniper woodland. Ancient Indian farmers did not practice irrigation. Dry farming required a delicately balanced climate—one that provided enough rainfall and yet enough warmth and sunshine to allow the corn, beans and squash to mature. This zone provided both. The small shrine next to the trail is also typical of many that dot the plateau. The larger shrine, however, is unusual.

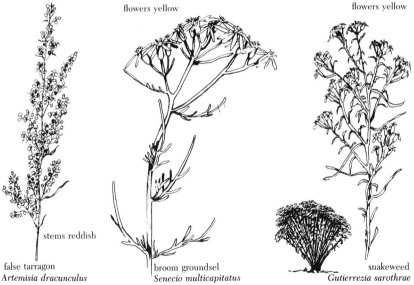

flowers yellow

flowers yellow

stems reddish

false tarragon
Artemisia dracunculus

broom groundsel
Senecio multicapitatus

snakeweed
Gutierrezia sarothrae

Three common shrubs that are indicators of overgrazing. With the introduction of livestock by the Spanish conquerors in the sixteenth century, the fragile high-desert ecology was drastically altered.

bl

View from Tyuonyi Overlook. Tyuonyi is right center; Frey Trail descends left center. On the horizon are Montoso Peak (7,315 ft), upper left, and other vent cones of the Cerros del Rio volcanic field.

A short extension of the Tyuonyi Overlook Trail continues to the canyon rim. The view is exceptional. In addition to the beautiful pattern of Tyuonyi ruin, the panorama encompasses the entire area of settlement in the canyon. Look for the orchard and parts of the irrigation ditch, relics of the days of Judge Abbott and the Freys. Both lie just west of Tyuonyi. Indians cultivated fields where the Park Service buildings now sit. Down the canyon, walls of dark andesite close around the small gorge where the Rito de los Frijoles has cut passage to the Rio Grande. Beyond are vent cones of the Cerros del Rio volcanic field, with Montoso Peak prominent on the horizon.

To the southwest are the San Miguel Mountains. The sharp pinnacle is Boundary Peak; the west boundary of the monument runs directly over its summit. High point of the range is Saint Peter's Dome, site of a Forest Service fire lookout. The lookout sometimes appears as a bright speck glinting in the light of a low-lying sun. The peaks predate by four million years the tuff of the Pajarito Plateau. They were not covered when the ash flows swirled around them.

nighthawk

On a summer's evening violet-green swallows dart about the promontory at the tip of the mesa, pursuing flying insects. A larger bird of similar habits flies higher in the sky. This, the common nighthawk, has long, pointed wings sharply bent at the joints. White patches on the undersides of the wings are clearly visible. The tail is slightly forked. The bird often repeats a sharp nasal cry, but an even more distinctive sound is a peculiar whirr it makes by rapidly beating its wings during its diving courtship display. The sound is audible at a distance in the quiet of a Bandelier evening. The nighthawk is a member of a family of night-flying birds called goatsuckers. It was once believed that birds of this family milked goats during the night while the owners slept.

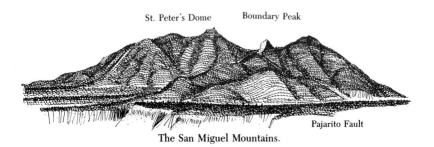

St. Peter's Dome   Boundary Peak

Pajarito Fault

The San Miguel Mountains.

37

BURNT MESA

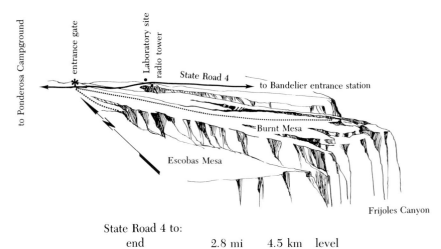

to Ponderosa Campground

entrance gate

Laboratory site
radio tower

State Road 4

to Bandelier entrance station

Burnt Mesa

Escobas Mesa

Frijoles Canyon

State Road 4 to:
end   2.8 mi   4.5 km   level

Burnt Mesa and Escobas Mesa together constitute a wedge that separates State Road 4 and Frijoles Canyon. The mesas are level, offering easy and undemanding hiking. They are flanked by rough canyons. A network of fire roads, closed to private vehicles, crosses the broad crowns. These roads are especially pleasant in early morning or on long summer evenings. In those rare years of heavy snowfall, they are fine cross-country ski routes.

The Burnt Mesa fire road starts at a gate in the monument fence on State Road 4 at a point about 2 miles east of Ponderosa Campground and 4.2 miles west of the main monument entrance. About a hundred feet beyond the gate the fire road branches. The left fork is the route of greater interest.

Burnt Mesa deserves its name. It has a history of periodic fires and was badly burned in La Mesa Fire of 1977. The frequency of fires here may account for an interesting anomaly: although most ancient Indian dwellings were located in pinyon-juniper woodland, Burnt Mesa, lying in the ponderosa forest, has a heavy concentration of ruins. The fires probably kept the mesa clear of thick vegetation and returned nutrients to the soil, making it suitable for agriculture.

The period of Indian occupation was between A.D. 1150 and 1600. Though none of the ruins here approach Tyuonyi in size, they are larger than the one- or two-room small-house sites that dot the mesas to the south. Many Burnt Mesa houseblocks contain storage rooms, indicating that they were occupied year-round. (In contrast, farmers on the lower mesas apparently lived near their fields in summer but retreated to the large pueblos during the winter months.)

Sites on Burnt Mesa lie fairly close to one another, though it seems unlikely they were all occupied at the same time. Relatively little archeological investigation has been done here.

The present condition of Burnt Mesa is a graphic lesson in fire ecology. Wildfires may not completely destroy a forest. Often, for reasons associated with microterrain and weather patterns, small islands of trees are left alive within a sea of blackened trunks. Studies show that the frequency of fires in an area determines how badly it will be burned in succeeding fires. Repeated low-intensity fires reduce the fuel load beneath the trees to levels that cannot sustain a blaze or carry it from tree to tree. In Bandelier National Monument the optimum fire frequency is 17 years. For many decades, however, the

Park Service pursued a policy of total fire suppression. By the time of La Mesa Fire some areas had not burned since 1878. When fire did come, it was devastating, destroying most of the ponderosa pine forests of the monument. The Park Service now conducts continuing research to determine when and where to use fire as a management tool.

Beneath the blackened, skeletal trees of Burnt Mesa is a thick carpet of grass. Immediately after La Mesa Fire, the Forest Service seeded grass in order to retard erosion during the summer thundershower season. Five species of grass were seeded, but one, slender wheatgrass, thrived to the exclusion of the others. The fire also stimulated growth of some indigenous grasses. Several patches of big bluestem stand beside the

On Burnt Mesa, groves of pines thrive amidst fallen logs, remnants of the fire of 1977. bl

39

Burnt Mesa fire road. This species, also called turkeyfoot, was rare in the monument until after the fire. Then thick stands suddenly sprouted and grew over six feet tall, spurred on by nutrients released from the burned vegetation. The mesa is beginning to recover now, and in isolated spots other native grasses—mountain muhly, mutton grass, hairy dropseed, and the three-awns—are returning.

The fields of Burnt Mesa once blazed with wildflowers. Where slender wheatgrass has not taken over, wildflowers still bloom. In July, the mesas glow with blue lupines (Texas bluebonnets), red Indian paintbrush, and yellow greenthreads. Greenthreads make excellent tea. Two species are common on the Pajarito Plateau. Navajo tea has bright yellow ray flowers (the "petals" of a daisy-like blossom). Cota, the other greenthread, lacks ray flowers; only the central disc flowers are present. Both plants have distinctive threadlike leaves and the blossoms have peculiar involucres with two sets of bracts. Cota was used medicinally by the Indians as a diuretic, as an arthritis remedy, and for blood complaints.

Burnt Mesa is a wintering ground for elk that summer in the valleys of the Jemez Caldera. From autumn to early spring elk tracks and droppings are numerous. In many places the tall grass is flattened where the elk have bedded. The animals stay hidden by day, but are often spotted along State Road 4 by early morning or late evening motorists. These elk, *Cervus elaphus*, were introduced

big bluestem
Andropogon gerardii

hairy
dropseed
*Blepharoneuron
tricholepis*

slender
wheatgrass
*Agropyron
trachycaulum*

Aristida fendleriana

Some common grasses of the Pajarito Plateau.

flowers blue

lupine
Lupinus sp.

flowers yellow

involucre

greenthread
Thelesperma trifidum

flowers red

Indian paintbrush
Castilleja integra

Red Indian paintbrush, yellow green-thread and blue lupines dot the mesas in summer.

here from the Yellowstone region in 1948. The original New Mexico elk herds were hunted to extinction at the turn of the century. Elk are presently increasing in number in northern New Mexico while deer populations have declined.

Both are important game animals.

Mule deer are found throughout the monument area, and sometimes roam the canyons and mesas during the day. Named for the size of their ears, *Odocoileus hemionus* (the name derives from Greek words meaning "hollow-toothed mule") inhabits most of western North America. Mule deer run in springy, stiff-legged bounds that seem awkward on level ground, but are efficient and effective for rapid uphill climbing.

The lower end of Burnt Mesa grades from ponderosa pine into pinyon-juniper unscarred by fire. It still bears an impressive collection of ruins. The fire road fades away at a point overlooking a maze of secondary canyons about a half-mile short of the rim of Frijoles Canyon itself.

bl

Blackened trunks and tall wheatgrass dominated the mesas soon after the fire. The trees are breaking in the wind now and the wheatgrass is retreating.

APACHE SPRING TRAIL

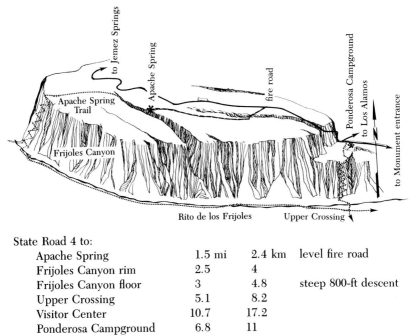

State Road 4 to:

Apache Spring	1.5 mi	2.4 km	level fire road
Frijoles Canyon rim	2.5	4	
Frijoles Canyon floor	3	4.8	steep 800-ft descent
Upper Crossing	5.1	8.2	
Visitor Center	10.7	17.2	
Ponderosa Campground	6.8	11	

This trail through upper Frijoles Canyon is in the mixed-conifer association, with a cool mountain climate. The canyon floor is a jungle of forest shade plants. Compared to the typical Southwest landscape of most of the monument, upper Frijoles seems to be a different world.

Access to the trailhead at Apache Spring is by Fire Road 3, which branches from State Road 4 at a point up the scarp 1.7 miles west of Ponderosa Campground. The road is closed to private vehicles, but the two-mile walk is pleasant and undemanding. A number of old logging roads, built long before the National Park Service acquired the area in 1963, branch away from the fire road. They make delightful cross-country ski routes in a snowy winter. The mesa was burned in the fire of 1977 and is in a classic rejuvenation phase. Aspen, the pioneer plant in the natural succession leading to the climax fir forest, sprouts in open clearings.

Apache Spring is one of a number of small springs lying at the zone of contact between the dacite core of the Jemez Mountains and the overlying welded tuff. The spring once served cattle and sheep drives from the Española Valley to the summer pastures of the *valles*. It was developed and encased in concrete and rock as part of the CCC project of 1935–37. The spring is located in the small canyon near the trailhead. A pipe once led from the spring to a concrete trough which has since been demolished by vandals.

The trail from Apache Spring to the rim of Frijoles Canyon is fairly level. The ponderosa pine forest here is recovering well from the fire. In summer the way is strewn with ripe wild strawberries, and forest birds sing in the trees. From the rim the trail drops sharply 800 feet to the canyon floor, switching across fragile slopes of pumice. Gullies have formed in this steep wall where hikers have repeatedly cut across the switchbacks. This graphically illustrates the reason for the admonition: stay on the trail.

At the end of the descent, the floor of Frijoles Canyon is wide and flat. Grassy meadows skirt the watercourse, alternating with stands of Douglas fir so dense that from within one scarcely realizes that this is the bottom of a deep

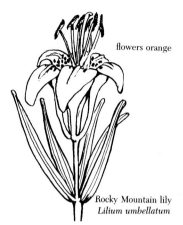

flowers orange

Rocky Mountain lily
Lilium umbellatum

canyon. Everywhere there is a riot of forest plants. Outstanding is the Rocky Mountain lily, blooming in July with a vibrant orange flower. It is an endangered species due to thoughtless collecting. In autumn aspen leaves carpet the path like gold coins.

bl

A few small meadows dot the aspen-mixed conifer forest near Apache Spring. This area offers cross-country skiing in winter.

43

dh

Aspen, ponderosa pine, Douglas fir and nodding brome grass crowd the floor of upper Frijoles Canyon.

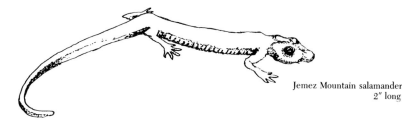

Jemez Mountain salamander
2″ long

Half a mile downstream are sturdy remains of a beaver dam. Its builders have long since moved away, and the stream has broken through the dam to drain the former pond. The canyon floor here is now a morass thick with cattails. Earthworks are still visible under a line of alders.

The trail continues 2.7 miles downstream to Upper Crossing. The forest gradually changes from mixed fir to ponderosa pine. Watch out for nettles and poison ivy. For the most part, this and the rest of the canyon escaped the 1977 fire but suffered from flooding soon af-

terward. It is now rehealing. From Upper Crossing it is 1.7 miles and a 400-foot climb to Ponderosa Campground, or 6 miles further downstream to the visitor center.

The rare and endangered Jemez Mountains salamander, *Plethodon neomexicanus*, has been found in upper Frijoles Canyon. This small amphibian, scarcely three inches long, lives in moist litter and rockfalls above 8,000 feet. It is restricted to the Jemez Mountains. To protect its habitat, the Park Service prohibits camping in the canyon west of Upper Crossing.

dh

bl

Indian trails like these at Tsankawi are found throughout the Pajarito Plateau.

Hikes in the
DETACHED
SECTION

Off of State Road 4, 11.5 miles northeast of the monument entrance, lies a detached section of Bandelier National Monument. Atop an imposing mesa is the site of an unexcavated Tewa ruin, rich in cliff dwellings and petroglyphs. Nearby are remains of a small area briefly occupied in the early part of this century. Both are short hikes, especially pleasant in the evening.

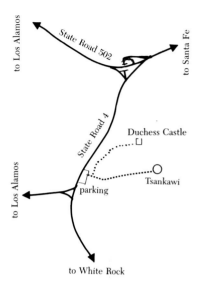

TSANKAWI

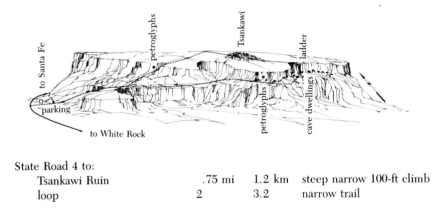

State Road 4 to:

Tsankawi Ruin	.75 mi	1.2 km	steep narrow 100-ft climb
loop	2	3.2	narrow trail

The trail to Tsankawi Ruin begins at State Road 4 near its junction with the truck route to Los Alamos. An informal parking lot and visitor shelter mark the entrance. A detailed pamphlet available at the trailhead describes many points of interest along the route. The walk provides a good introduction to the lower Pajarito Plateau and its prehistoric Indian life.

47

The trail follows narrow Indian paths up the side of Tsankawi Mesa. Similar trails have been worn into the soft tuff throughout the entire plateau. Atop the mesa the unexcavated ruin occupies a commanding site. The ground plan is still discernible; two kivas were located within a plaza and several others lie outside the houseblock. Tsankawi was the home of Tewa-speaking people. The San Ildefonso Indians claim it to be one of their ancestral villages. It was apparently occupied between 1150 and 1600. *Tsankawi* is a Tewa word meaning "gap of the sharp, round cactus."

A trail skirts the south-facing cliff of Tsankawi Mesa, passing a series of cave dwellings. This alternate return route requires a short descent by ladder, and the trail is narrow and precarious in places. The wealth of dwellings and petroglyphs along the route is typical of many of the south-facing cliffs in the Tewa section of the Pajarito Plateau.

The cliffside overlooks the broad canyon bottom where farming sustained the dense populations of Classic Phase times. The ruins of three other large pueblos lie within a two-mile radius of Tsankawi, all contemporaneous with it. The surrounding mesas are strewn with the remains of smaller dwellings. The lands adjacent to Tsankawi Mesa are either part of the San Ildefonso Indian Reservation or belong to the Department of Energy–Los Alamos National Laboratory. All are closed to the public.

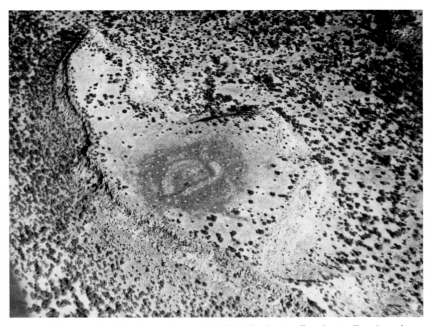

Aerial photograph of Tsankawi taken in 1929 by Charles Lindbergh. Lindbergh made aerial surveys of many archeological sites throughout the Southwest. *Collections of the Museum of New Mexico. Neg. #70.1/239 L.112*

DUCHESS CASTLE

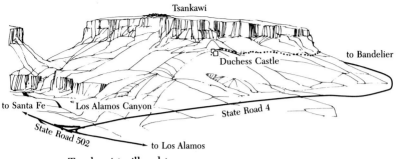

Tsankawi

Duchess Castle

to Bandelier

to Santa Fe — Los Alamos Canyon

State Road 4

State Road 502 — to Los Alamos

Tsankawi trailhead to:
Duchess Castle

0.75 mi   1.1 km

On the broad floor of Los Alamos Canyon just north of Tsankawi Mesa lie the ruins of a small compound known locally as "Duchess Castle." Its builder, Madame Vera von Blumenthal, was not a duchess but apparently did belong to the minor Russian nobility. She had come to the United States to promote interest in Russian handicrafts in this country. In 1917, she and her friend Miss Rose Dugan (or Dougan) obtained a permit from the Forest Service to build a summer home here. The house they built was not large but was substantially constructed. Visiting guests from Santa Fe referred to it as "The Fort."

It is illegal under the Antiquities Act of 1906 and the Cultural Resources Protection Act of 1978 to collect potshęrds. They are a primary method of dating archeological sites.

Rose Dugan was well-to-do and an ardent aviatrix, but shy and sickly. She and Madame von Blumenthal spent only the warmer months of the year on the Pajarito Plateau, preferring to winter in Pasadena, California.

Although seventeenth-century Spanish chroniclers had commented on the excellence of the native pottery, by 1900 much of the art had been lost. Both ladies were sincerely interested in the crafts of the Indians and, when in residence, tried to encourage the local potters to improve the quality of their wares. Because they spent only a few months here each year, however, they accomplished little until Madame von Blumenthal asked archeologist Edgar Lee Hewett to take over the project and provided him with an allowance for that purpose. Hewett honored the trust. He and his assistant Kenneth Chapman encouraged Indian artisans, suggested improvements and, most importantly, found markets for Indian work. Under this guidance its quality improved markedly. Today pottery produced at San Ildefonso and Santa Clara Pueblos is world famous.

Entrance to Duchess Castle is at the Tsankawi trailhead; the trail skirts the west end of Tsankawi Mesa. Only concrete foundations and crumbling walls remain. The castle lies at the edge of a large field, and one might assume that the ladies did some farming. Instead, the field proves to be the site of an ancient Indian ruin of unusual design. In contrast to the houseblock enclosing a plaza, as at Tsankawi, this complex had a low wall enclosing a large courtyard. The eastern end was obliterated by the castle construction.

bl

The ruins of Duchess Castle sit amidst the sagebrush near the Los Alamos turnoff on State Road 4.

Wilderness trails
originating at the
VISITOR CENTER

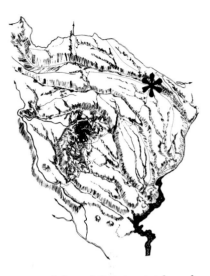

Four of the five trails that traverse the mesas between Frijoles and Capulin canyons are best approached from the Visitor Center. (The fifth starts at Ponderosa Campground.) The Frijolito Trail climbs out of Frijoles Canyon and leads to a medium-sized ruin atop the mesa. From there the Lower Alamo Trail goes to a small archeological area at the mouth of Alamo Canyon. The Stone Lions Trail provides access to two of the major features of Bandelier National Monument: Yapashi Pueblo and the Shrine of the Stone Lions. West Alamo Trail connects the Stone Lions and Lower Alamo trails.

None of these hikes is trivial; each begins with a 500-foot climb out of Frijoles Canyon. Two require the strenuous crossing of 500-foot deep Alamo Canyon.

bl

Summer thundershowers are common on the Pajarito Plateau.

FRIJOLITO TRAIL

Visitor Center to:
    Frijolito Ruin   .75 mi   1.2 km   steep 500-ft ascent

Across the Rito de los Frijoles from the Visitor Center, behind the picnic area comfort station, Frijolito Trail begins its zigzag up the steep south wall of the canyon. Though this ascent is more strenuous than the leisurely climb provided by the Stone Lions Trail, the view into Frijoles Canyon is striking. After only a few switchbacks, the hiker is rewarded by a splendid overview of Tyuonyi flanked by numerous cave dwellings on the opposite canyon wall. The Frey Trail, descending the north wall, is clearly visible, as is the cluster of Park Service buildings built in the 1930s. Up the canyon to the west vertical cliffs frame the grassy south slope of Pajarito Mountain on the rim of the Jemez (Valles) Caldera.

Although Frijolito Trail undoubtedly follows an Indian path that connected Frijolito and Tyuonyi, it is not the route that Adolph Bandelier followed when he entered the canyon in the 1880s. That trail lies abandoned and filled with rubble about half a mile down the canyon. Still, a present-day visitor can appreciate Bandelier's feelings when he wrote in his journal: "About 4 P.M. the border of the almost precipitous descent into the Cañón de los Frijoles was reached, and it took one-half hour to descend—on foot, of course. The

dh

Tyuonyi and the cliff dwellings as seen from the Frijolito Trail.

A seemingly endless series of switchbacks ascend the south wall of Frijoles Canyon to Frijolito Ruin. **bl**

grandest thing I ever saw. A magnificent growth of pines, encina, alamos, and towering cliffs, of pumice or volcanic tuff, exceedingly friable."*

Frijolito Ruin lies on a slight rise near the rim of Frijoles Canyon. The village was contemporaneous with Tyuonyi, built between 1350 and 1500. Little is known of the lifestyle of the mesa people or of their relations with Tyuonyi people. Edgar Lee Hewett partially excavated the site in 1908, but left little recorded information about it. Its name, "little bean," was given to it at that time by Hewett's colleague A. V. Kidder.

From Frijolito Ruin the Lower Alamo Trail branches to the south (left). Frijolito Trail itself contin-

Lange and Riley, *The Southwestern Journals.* p. 165

ues west for about a mile to join Stone Lions Trail. About halfway between the two points, watch for the lone alligator juniper tree on the south side of the trail.

bl

A broken metate, used for grinding grain, lies center right amid the brick-shaped rubble at Frijolito Ruin. Note the double row of tuff blocks left center where the wall toppled intact.

53

LOWER ALAMO TRAIL

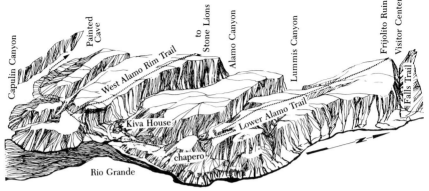

Capulin Canyon · Painted Cave · West Alamo Rim Trail · to Stone Lions · Alamo Canyon · Lummis Canyon · Frijolito Ruin · Visitor Center · Falls Trail · Kiva House · Lower Alamo Trail · chapero · Rio Grande

Visitor Center to:

	mi	km	
Lummis Canyon	5	8	carry water
Alamo Canyon	6.4	10.2	

From Frijolito Ruin, Lower Alamo Trail leads south across the barren mesas to the mouth of Alamo Canyon and the Rio Grande in White Rock Canyon. The trail is new, built by the Park Service in 1978, but the route is ancient. Said Adolph Bandelier in his *Final Report* (1892), "Across this mesa a trail from east to west, formerly much used by the Navajo Indians on their incursions against the Spanish and Pueblo settlements, creeps up from the Rio Grande, and, crossing the mesa, rises to the crest of the mountains. It seems almost impossible for cattle and horses to ascend the dizzy slope, yet the savages more than once have driven their living booty with merciless haste over this trail to their distant homes."* Bandelier himself first entered his namesake area on this trail. In later years he guided Charles Lummis across the mesas. The incurably romantic

Lummis was enchanted. Wrote he, "It was hot, our loads were heavy and the climbing heavier yet as we made our way up 1,000 foot cliffs, trudging across mesas, descended into wild cañons, across and up other cliffs. But we were happy as schoolboys. The dry wine of the high air filled us down to our diaphragms and everywhere the eye rejoiced with noble beauty."* Bandelier carried his portfolio of maps and notes, his transit and surveying materials. Lummis carried his camera equipment and photographic plates, weighing altogether thirty to forty pounds. This was the only route from the south into Frijoles Canyon known to Bandelier.

It is a long five miles across the mesa to the rim of White Rock Canyon. The scraggly pinyon-juniper woodland may seem monotonous and dull. But the trail is exposed to all the wonderful va-

Bandelier, *Final Report.* p. 147

Fiske and Lummis, *Charles F. Lummis.* p. 63

sandhill crane
gray   37" long

garies of the high-desert weather and the view is splendid in all directions. To the east, at the border of the Rio Grande Rift, are the Sangre de Cristo Mountains, the giant tail of the Rockies, half hidden by the little cones of the Cerros del Rio volcanic field. To the south, 35 air-miles away, is Sandia Mountain, a tilted uplift of 1.4-billion-year-old Precambrian granite that also borders the rift. At its base, usually hidden in smog, is Albuquerque. To the southwest, only four miles away, are the San Miguel Mountains. Northwest is the east rim of Jemez Caldera, source of the ash flows that formed the Pajarito Plateau. Connecting the two ranges is a long scarp called the Pajarito Fault. The conical lump halfway between them is Rabbit Hill, an intrusive volcanic vent that predated the tuff ash flows by ten million years.

In February and again in November these lower mesas are magical, for then sandhill cranes fly between nesting grounds in Idaho and winter homes on game refuges near Socorro. The flocks are a grand sight as the birds soar upward on thermals above White Rock Canyon, then regroup into V-shaped formation before continuing their journey. The cranes' distinctive calls unmistakably herald the change in the seasons.

In summer, look for showy four o'clock, a sprawling plant with gray-green leaves and brilliant purple blossoms. The plant justly deserves its scientific name *Mirabilis multiflora*. The flowers are without petals; showy parts are colored sepals. Several flowers together are held in a little green cup of bracts. The flowers bloom in subdued light, generally in the evening, giving them the common name "four o'clock." Here on the mesa they bloom in the dense shade of a pinyon or juniper at other times of day.

At the end of the mesa the trail descends a low tuff bluff onto a terrace of Cerros del Rio deposits, following an old sheep route past

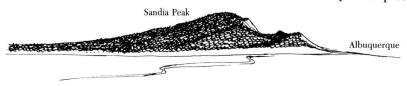

Sandia Peak

Albuquerque

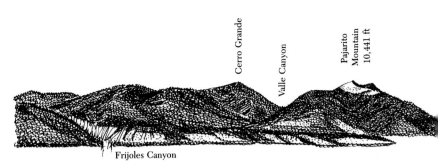

Cerro Grande

Valle Canyon

Pajarito Mountain 10,441 ft

Frijoles Canyon

pillars of basalt down to a narrow saddle of pumice. To the east, 600 feet below, lies the Rio Grande in White Rock Canyon. To the west, 300 feet below, is Lummis Canyon. To the south, 100 feet above, is an isolated mesa which Adolph Bandelier called the *Chapero* "slouch hat." In his *Final Report*, Bandelier graphically describes communal hunts held by the Indians of Cochiti and Santo Domingo at this spot. Hunters drove game up the Chapero and over its precipitous sides to their deaths. One of the prey mentioned by Bandelier was mountain sheep, presumably the Rocky Mountain bighorn, *Ovis canadensis*. He reported seeing one in Frijoles Canyon in the year 1880, but by 1890 that animal had disappeared from

the Jemez.

From the saddle the trail descends into Lummis Canyon and proceeds to Alamo Canyon. The mouth of Alamo lies on the floodplain of Cochiti Lake. Dead skeletons of junipers, pinyons, cottonwoods and pines dot the mudflats. Annual weeds—tumbleweeds, amaranths, and lamb's quarters—now thrive there.

Prior to the filling of Cochiti Lake, the Park Service contracted for intensive archeological study

bl

Hexagonal cracks form a bizarre paving on the mudflats of Cochiti Lake.

flowers purple-pink

showy four o'clock

Mirabilis multiflora

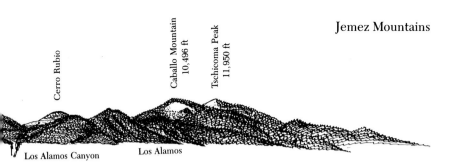

Cerro Rubio

Caballo Mountain 10,496 ft

Tschicoma Peak 11,950 ft

Los Alamos Canyon   Los Alamos

at the mouth of Alamo Canyon and elsewhere in lower White Rock Canyon. The excavations gave evidence of human occupation dating back to 1750 B.C. Archaic Indians came here only seasonally, camping on sand dunes beside the Rio Grande. Since they had not developed pottery, they cooked food by dropping heated stones into watertight baskets, an adequate method for preparing mush or stew. Such heated stones often shattered from the extreme temperature change and were discarded beside the firepit. Arrowheads, knife fragments and other flaking debris were also strewn about the campsites. These people did not build permanent dwellings, but probably constructed temporary shelters near their hearths. They were primarily hunter-gatherers.

Archeologists found little evidence of human occupation be-

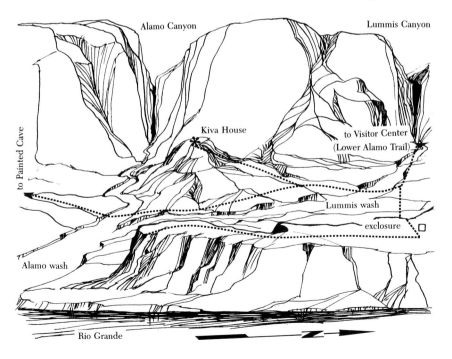

Alamo Canyon

Lummis Canyon

to Painted Cave

Kiva House

to Visitor Center (Lower Alamo Trail)

Lummis wash

exclosure

Alamo wash

Rio Grande

bl

bl

Two views of Kiva House.

tween 590 B.C. and A.D. 1175, when Indian farmers first appeared in this area. Many sites subsequently were occupied on low bluffs beside the Lummis and Alamo streambeds. Agricultural terraces were constructed across small drainages. Dwellings ranged in size from one room to a houseblock of perhaps eight rooms accompanied by a small kiva. Kiva House, a larger ruin located on a low ridge overlooking the confluence of the two washes, has been stabilized following excavation. The presence of storage rooms indicates that this and many other houseblocks were occupied year-round.

At low water, the hiker can continue south to Capulin Canyon, switching 400 feet up the steep wall of White Rock Canyon as it leaves the lower Alamo basin. On October 23, 1880, Adolph Bandelier was led down this trail during his first trip to Frijoles Canyon. The description he wrote then is as valid now: "In some places the descents are terrible and cannot be made on horseback. The lava is reached north of the Potrero Chiato, and thence on to the banks of the Cañon del Norte which is reached by a horrible descent. [The descent here is through] ugly, black, cutting, ringing lava blocks."* But the view of Cañón del Norte (White Rock Canyon) is ample reward. Bandelier's black Chapero rises across the arid basin, flanked on the west by the beautiful orange cliff which separates Alamo and Lummis canyons. Kiva House sits on its barren ridge. Flanking the top of the trail is a band of sedimentary deposits, remains of an ancient lake that filled White Rock Canyon long before the ash flows. East of the Rio Grande, the dark cliff of the Cerros del Rio volcanic field is broken only by the gash of Arroyo Montoso. Said Adolph Bandelier in his *Final Report* of 1892: "The whole country is a wilderness and will scarcely become anything else."°

* Lange and Riley, *The Southwestern Journals.* p. 164

° Bandelier, *Final Report.* p. 149

dh

59

STONE LIONS TRAIL

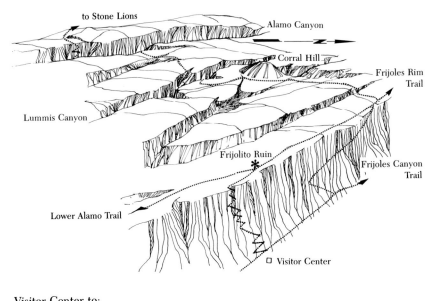

to Stone Lions

Alamo Canyon

Corral Hill

Frijoles Rim Trail

Lummis Canyon

Frijolito Ruin

Frijoles Canyon Trail

Lower Alamo Trail

□ Visitor Center

Visitor Center to:

	mi	km	
Corral Hill	2	3.2	400-ft climb
Alamo Canyon, north rim	3	4.8	carry water
Yapashi Ruin	5.5	8	
Shrine of the Stone Lions	6	8.9	
Capulin Canyon	7	10.5	

The trail to Corral Hill and Stone Lions branches west (right) from Frijolito Trail behind the comfort station in the Frijoles Canyon picnic area. It proceeds west on the canyon floor for a quarter mile or so, then ascends by a long, leisurely climb up the south wall to the canyon rim, and finally turns south into the Bandelier Wilderness.

On both this and Frijolito Trail the dry hillside is graced by a surprising variety of flowering shrubs. In early spring the first buds to open are those of currants and

gooseberries. Look for their small, trumpet-shaped flowers. A few weeks later both foul-smelling blossoms and shiny green leaflets in sets of three appear on the hop trees. In early June, New Mexico locust blooms with spectacular bouquets of pink blossoms. In summer, fragrant mock-orange and lacy mountain spray flowers cover otherwise nondescript, shrubby plants.

From either trail, watch the canyon birds as they go about their tasks. By day, large black ravens and turkey vultures soar past the canyon walls searching for carrion. At night, the vultures fly in to roost in the cottonwood trees of Frijoles Canyon. Except in winter, flocks of smaller birds fly over the treetops. Two species are similar in habits and appearance but are unrelated to each other. White-throated swifts have black-and-white markings on their undersides and a "twinkling" mode of flight. Swifts belong to the order *Apodiformes*, "without feet." The birds, of course, do have feet, but all four of the toes point forward. Swifts cannot perch on horizontal objects such as limbs or wires, but must cling to a vertical surface to

vulture

raven

Vultures fly with their wings held in a broad V. Ravens have wedge-shaped tails.

rest. Swifts are closely related to hummingbirds.

Violet-green swallows usually fly with the swifts. They have iridescent green backs and wholly white underparts. Swallows belong to the large order *Passeriformes*, the perching or song birds, a group that includes, among many others,

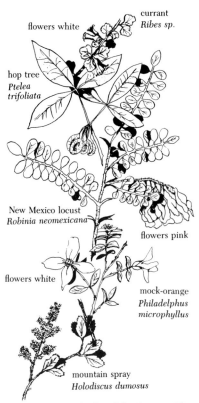

currant
Ribes sp.

flowers white

hop tree
*Ptelea
trifoliata*

New Mexico locust
Robinia neomexicana

flowers pink

flowers white

mock-orange
*Philadelphus
microphyllus*

mountain spray
Holodiscus dumosus

Some common shrubs of the Pajarito Plateau.

white-throated swift

violet-green swallow

to Upper Crossing
the "Y"
Frijoles Rim Trail
Upper Alamo Trail
Frijoles Canyon
to Visitor Center
to Frijolito Ruin
Lummis Canyon
Stone Lions Trail

robins, sparrows, mockingbirds and ravens. Violet-green swallows range along the Pacific coast as far north as Alaska, but are also found throughout the arid, inland West. Both swallows and swifts feed on insects they catch in flight.

Near the top of the trail, look to the northwest across Frijoles Canyon to see several long ladders leading to Ceremonial Cave. Atop the mesa the trail soon is joined by the trail from Frijolito Ruin to the east. A few yards beyond this junction the trail again divides. The Stone Lions Trail turns south (left). Continuing to the west is the Frijoles Rim Trail. It joins the Upper Alamo Trail at the "Y" 3.5 miles away.

At the crest of the next gentle rise several trees grow on a low mound of rubble. This is the ruin of a small house. Hundreds like this dot the Pajarito Plateau. Many were temporary farmsteads used only during the growing season. In winter the inhabitants moved back to the large pueblos. It appears that these small houses were not occupied for long periods—a few years or a generation at most. The ancient farmers had no knowledge of soil building or fertilization and were forced to move when the soil became so depleted of nutrients that their crops no longer would grow. Soil analysis shows these fields to be low in nutrients to the present day.

dh

Tuff columns of Frijoles Canyon frame the ladders to Ceremonial Cave, center.

62

Scattered tuff blocks mark ruins of the Pajarito Plateau.

Continuing south, the trail crosses a rough little canyon. Note a line of stones or a tree limb buried across the trail at intervals. These objects are waterbars, designed to divert water from rain or melting snow.

A mile beyond the rim of Frijoles Canyon lies Corral Hill, a low symmetrical mound on the gently undulating mesa. An ancient corral stands nearby. Camps and corrals were scattered throughout the monument area from land-grant days into the 1930s, serving shepherds, cattlemen, forest rangers and "dudes."

In the area between Frijoles and Alamo Canyons the trail traverses a boundary separating pinyon-juniper and ponderosa associations. Each species is at the limits of its range. Stresses caused by recent changes in climatic conditions weakened the pines, and an in-festation of bark beetles killed many of them. The trees' skeletons remain strewn in the open forest. This area escaped La Mesa Fire of 1977.

The grasses found here are more characteristic of mesa vegetation than the slender wheatgrass of Burnt Mesa. The lacy grass with delicate awns is mountain muhly, dominant grass species of the ponderosa pine forest. It is one member of the large genus of western range grasses named in honor of Gotthilf Heinrich Ernst Muhlenberg, a Pennsylvania-born Lutheran pastor and botanist of the late eighteenth century. Rangers have long called all grasses of the genus, "muhly." The name has nothing to do with mules.

Little bluestem, *Andropogon scoparius* ("broomlike man's beard"), blooms in late summer when it can be recognized by its

A corral near Corral Hill. Several corrals and line camp sites remain in the monument. b1

shining, silky seedheads and rust-colored stems. Together with its relative, big bluestem, this species made up the great grasslands of the prairie states. Bluestem is a newcomer to this area. The pollen is not found in the stratified debris of archeological sites.

A distinctive plant of disturbed areas is candlestick plant or mullein, sometimes called flannel plant. A native of Europe, it is now established in the temperate zone throughout the world. Mullein has a long history of use as a medicinal plant, principally for disorders of the upper respiratory system. Indians smoked the dried leaves to relieve lung troubles. Pioneers soaked the stout spikes in fat or wax and used them as torches. Mullein is biennial, living the first year as a low rosette of large, grayish leaves. The second year it shoots to a height of six feet, flow-

ers, and then dies. Be sure to feel the flannel-like leaves, and note the tiny, star-shaped hairs that cover the plant.

About a quarter-mile beyond Corral Hill the Stone Lions Trail descends 120 feet into Lummis Canyon. Lummis is a multibranched canyon draining the broad mesa separating Frijoles and Alamo Canyons. At its lower end it rivals those canyons in size, but here it is a network of sinuous, fingerlike ravines.

A mile beyond Lummis Canyon, the trail tops a gentle rise and arrives at the brink of Alamo Canyon. A great gash in the plateau, 500 feet deep and scarcely a quarter-mile wide, Alamo is a splendid sight, well worth a trip in itself. The trail becomes a majestic staircase, descending the steep slope, then in a seemingly endless ribbon of stairs, climbs the opposite

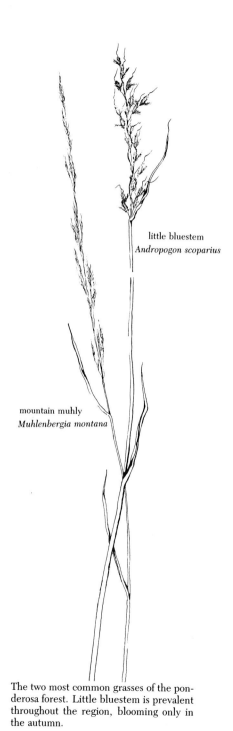

little bluestem
Andropogon scoparius

mountain muhly
Muhlenbergia montana

The two most common grasses of the ponderosa forest. Little bluestem is prevalent
throughout the region, blooming only in
the autumn.

mullein
Verbascum thapsus

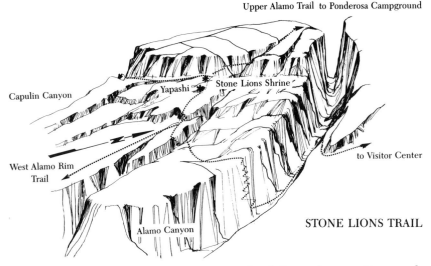

Capulin Canyon

Yapashi

Stone Lions Shrine

West Alamo Rim
Trail

to Visitor Center

Alamo Canyon

STONE LIONS TRAIL

wall. South of Alamo Canyon the vegetation changes dramatically. Gone are the tall pines; ahead is the so-called pygmy forest of pinyon and juniper. Much of the surface is unweathered tuff interspersed with shallow pockets

bl

Hikers ascend the Grand Staircase out of Alamo Canyon.

of soil. Beneath stunted trees only snakeweed and prickly pear cactus are abundant. The trail dips briefly into a small tributary of Alamo Canyon and then climbs a gentle slope. The West Alamo Rim Trail branches south to White Rock Canyon 3.5 miles away. A mile further west on the Stone Lions Trail is the ruin of Yapashi Pueblo.

One of the largest ruins on the Pajarito Plateau, Yapashi now consists of mounds of rubble thickly grown with cholla cactus. The pueblo was a large crescent, about one hundred feet long, opening to the southwest. An isolated houseblock stood to the south. The pueblo was multistoried. The outlines of several kivas are clearly visible; pinyons have taken root in the soft soil that fills them. Little is known of the history of Yapashi. Edgar Hewett ran a single trench through a part of the ruin in 1908. He gives occupancy dates of 1200 to 1475. The Cochiti Indians regard the pueblo as one of their ancient homes. The word *Yapashi*,

500-foot-deep Alamo Canyon. Stone Lions Trail descends the cliff near the center of this dh view.

View of the mesa near Yapashi Pueblo ruin. At the time of occupation, all trees had dh been cut for firewood. Indians farmed in small pockets of soil in sheltered spots, usually growing only a few plants in each plot.

The walls of Yapashi Pueblo stood higher in 1898 when Charles Lummis took this photograph. *Lummis Collection, UNM General Library, Special Collections Dept.*

Yapashi Pueblo today. A forest of cane cholla cactus tops the rubble piles. Impressive bl
pinyons grow in the old kivas, which collect the available moisture.

Stone Lions Shrine in 1890. The enclosure is now surrounded by pinyons. There is at present no method of determining the age of the shrine. Photo by Charles Lummis. *Maxwell Museum of Anthropology, University of New Mexico.*

Deer antlers and pottery shards at the Shrine of the Stone Lions.

dh

"sacred enclosure," refers to nearby Stone Lions shrine. The Keres called the site *Mokatakowet-ka'matsesoma*, "pueblo ruin where the mountain lions lie."

A long half-mile beyond Yapashi is the Shrine of the Stone Lions. An enclosure of boulders surrounds two mountain lions carved into the tuff. Fine details of the carving have been obliterated, but the forms are still recognizable. The shrine served Indians from a large area, including the Keres, Tewa, and Jemez—even the Zuni far to the west. Indians from nearby pueblos still leave offerings at the shrine.

At Stone Lions the trail divides. One branch, the Upper Alamo Trail, leads west up the scarp of the Pajarito Fault and on to Upper Alamo Crossing and out to Ponderosa Campground, a distance of 7.4 miles. The second branch turns south (left) below the scarp and after a mile descends into Capulin Canyon, where it joins the Capulin trail network that provides access to Painted Cave, St. Peter's Dome and Cochiti Canyon far to the south. The easiest return to the Visitor Center is back on the Stone Lions Trail.

Charles Lummis and companion camp in the monument. *Collections of the Museum of New Mexico.*

WEST ALAMO RIM TRAIL

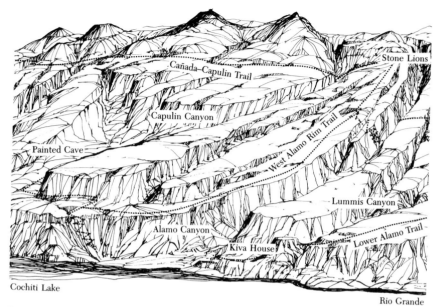

Cañada–Capulin Trail

Capulin Canyon

Stone Lions

West Alamo Rim Trail

Painted Cave

Lummis Canyon

Alamo Canyon

Kiva House

Lower Alamo Trail

Cochiti Lake

Rio Grande

Visitor Center to:

Stone Lions–West Alamo			
junction	4	mi	6.4 km	carry twice as much water
Kiva House (Alamo Canyon)	7.5		12.1	rough 700-ft descent

West Alamo Rim Trail branches south from the Stone Lions Trail about a mile beyond the west rim of Alamo Canyon. The junction is just west of the small tributary canyon that cuts the plateau here. It is a long and lonely tramp down the barren mesa in the heart of the Bandelier Wilderness to the Lower Alamo Trail three miles away. From this open highland the view is superb; the Pajarito Plateau stretches north to the mountainous rim of the caldera and west to the base of the San Miguel Mountains. To the east, Alamo Canyon drops 700 feet to a sandy bottom fringed with ponderosa pines. Other canyons in the mon-

ument appear only as ripples on a gently undulating plateau. To the east, cones of the Cerros del Rio block the view toward Santa Fe. Only the giant Sangre de Cristo Range rises above them.

The trail is new, built in 1980, but the route was old in 1880 when Adolph Bandelier first made his way to Stone Lions across this mesa, called Potrero de las Vacas (literally "cow pasture"). The origin of that name is obscure, as he did not mention seeing cattle. He did comment on bears, which climbed into pinyons and ripped off branches to get the edible nuts. The bears have since retreated to the mountains; today the mesas

71

support deer and burros.

In about a mile, the trail passes an exclosure—an area about 30 by 60 feet partitioned into three sections. One section is fully open; the second is fenced in such a way as to exclude large grazing animals. The third is fenced tightly enough to keep out animals of any size. The structure is used as part of a research effort by the Park Service to determine the impact of grazers on the mesa vegetation. Gone from this region is the diversity of grasses found on Burnt Mesa, or even at Corral Hill. Only little bluestem and blue grama have withstood heavy grazing by feral burros. Stunted plants, clipped to only inches, sit atop small pedestals of dirt left when the surrounding soil washed away.

On a sparkling winter day watch for mountain bluebirds which mi-

bluebird

grate to the lower mesas. The males are an electric blue; females are gray with blue on their wings and tail. The birds hover low over the ground searching for insects. Bluebirds tend to flock in winter, and a small area of the silent mesa can suddenly come alive with shimmering, hovering birds.

Animal exclosures are research devices to investigate the effects of various grazing animals bl
on high-desert vegetation. There are several exclosures within the monument.

At the lower end of the potrero the view opens onto White Rock Canyon and the little dell at the mouth of Alamo Canyon. Look for Kiva House on the juniper-dotted hillock near the Lummis-Alamo confluence. Bandelier's Chapero rises above the skeletal forest on the flood plain of Cochiti Lake and blocks the view to the north.

West Alamo Rim Trail is without question an arduous hike. But standing on this rocky headland, with the windswept mesa to the rear and the giant cleft of Alamo Canyon below, hearing the murmur of the Rio Grande and on a crystal autumn day the call of the sandhill cranes, one can but agree with Adolph Bandelier: it is all exceedingly grand.

The trail descends 300 feet through a rough and rocky little canyon to a bench where it joins the Lower Alamo Trail. Southward (right) that trail crosses Hondo Canyon and descends into Capulin Canyon. Painted Cave is about three miles away. Northward (left) about a quarter-mile is Adolph Bandelier's "horrible descent" down into White Rock Canyon. (This trail may be blocked by high waters of the lake.) It is a long 7.5 miles to the Visitor Center via the Lower Alamo Trail.

View from the rim of Alamo Canyon looking south to White Rock Canyon and the Rio Grande. Alamo Canyon is 900 feet deep at this point. b1

Trailhead at
PONDEROSA CAMPGROUND

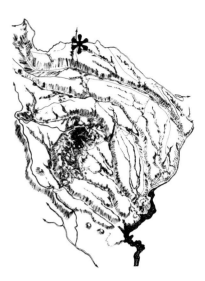

From Ponderosa Campground a short trail leads down to a fire road, which in turn heads south one mile to the rim of Frijoles Canyon. There a trail descends the north wall to Upper Crossing. From there trails lead downstream 5.6 miles to the Visitor Center and upstream 5.1 miles to Apache Spring. The Upper Alamo Trail climbs south out of the canyon and into the Bandelier Wilderness. Upper Crossing is a beautiful spot in the deep canyon amidst the tall conifers beside the sparkling Rito de los Frijoles. Many hikers with only a few hours to spare consider it a worthwhile destination in itself.

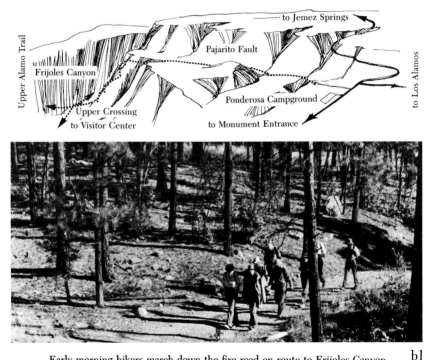

Early morning hikers march down the fire road en route to Frijoles Canyon. bl

74

UPPER ALAMO TRAIL

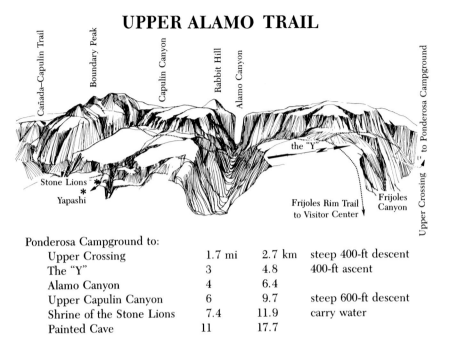

Cañada–Capulin Trail · Boundary Peak · Capulin Canyon · Rabbit Hill · Alamo Canyon · to Ponderosa Campground · the "Y" · Stone Lions · Yapashi · Frijoles Rim Trail to Visitor Center · Frijoles Canyon · Upper Crossing

Ponderosa Campground to:			
Upper Crossing	1.7 mi	2.7 km	steep 400-ft descent
The "Y"	3	4.8	400-ft ascent
Alamo Canyon	4	6.4	
Upper Capulin Canyon	6	9.7	steep 600-ft descent
Shrine of the Stone Lions	7.4	11.9	carry water
Painted Cave	11	17.7	

Upper Alamo Trail traverses the western end of the monument. Because of its high elevation, the route was thickly forested and suffered the most devastation from La Mesa Fire. The fire started on a narrow ridge between Frijoles and Alamo Canyons and swept down the mesa through an aged ponderosa pine forest filled with downed fuelwood. Now the mesas are covered with blackened, broken trees and a carpet of slender wheatgrass.

The route starts at Ponderosa Campground. A fire road traverses the level mesa one mile to the north rim of Frijoles Canyon. A well built but rough trail continues down the 400-foot north cliff to Upper Crossing, then immediately begins the long, slow climb up the south wall.

For the most part, the large canyons of the monument were spared the effects of the fire. This ascent is a pleasant one up a steep slope forested with ponderosa pine, white fir and Douglas fir. Douglas fir is not a true fir, nor is its former botanical name *Pseudotsuga taxifolia,* "false hemlock with yew-like leaves," very helpful. (The species has since been renamed *P. menziesii* in honor of botanist Archibald Menzies. Taxonomists seem to delight in namesmanship.) At one time or another the tree was classified as a true fir, a spruce, a hemlock, and even as a pine. In 1825, Scottish botanist David Douglas recognized that it required a genus of its own. The common name commemorates his work. Douglas fir supplies more lumber than any other tree in the

Pseudotsuga menziesii
Douglas fir

white fir
Abies concolor

a Douglas fir. Branches and twigs are used in ceremonial dances either as articles of clothing—collars, breastplates, belts, headdresses—or are carried by the dancers. After the ritual they are discarded ceremoniously in some sacred place. Douglas firs become large trees with deeply furrowed, grayish bark. They have distinctive cones which hang downward from the branches and are shed intact. A three-pointed bract ("Neptune's trident") protrudes from beneath the cone scales. The needles are single and rectangular in cross-section. They are high in vitamin C.

world and comprises some 60 percent of the standing timber in the West. Pueblo Indians consider the tree sacred, believing that mankind first climbed from the underworld to the earthly realm on

The trail from Upper Crossing south out of Frijoles Canyon is not steep, but it climbs relentlessly 400 feet to the mesa top and into the heart of La Mesa Fire area. Blackened trunks stand like broken

View near the "Y" three months after La Mesa Fire of 1977. The heat was so intense dh that sap boiled within the tree trunks and exploded bark from the trees.

Some trees were so completely incinerated that even the roots burned underground, bl leaving only rounded holes radiating from a central depression.

matchsticks, and the ground is littered with skeletal fallen treetops. Look for peculiar bowl-shaped depressions in the soil with small round tunnels radiating from them. These were locations of trees so incinerated that even the roots burned underground. In some areas the fire was so hot that sap in tree trunks flashed to steam. The resulting explosions blew the bark from the trees. No plant survived the fire here. When the ashes cooled the mesa was a stark monochrome of blacks and grays.

Life soon returned, and some of the pioneer plants still grow between the robust clumps of slender wheatgrass. Look for nodding onions with drooping heads of small lavender flowers. Soon after the fire the mesas glowed with masses of wild onion. Buckbrush, a low

sprawling bush with small green leaves and spiny branches, sprouted almost immediately after

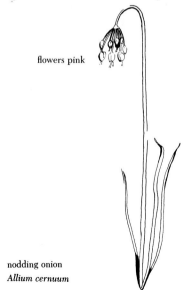

flowers pink

nodding onion
Allium cernuum

77

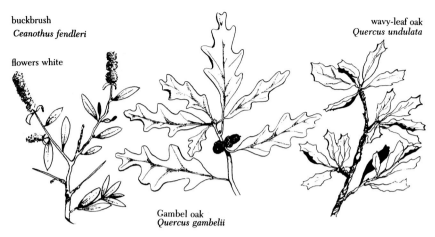

buckbrush
Ceanothus fendleri

flowers white

wavy-leaf oak
Quercus undulata

Gambel oak
Quercus gambelii

Three shrubs stimulated by fire. Buckbrush grows less than two feet tall. The oaks grow in thickets and can attain six feet.

the fire. In spring, buckbrush is covered with fragrant white blossoms that produce a lather if rubbed in water. As the name implies, deer browse the branches. Within days of the fire, oaks began sprouting from tough, fire-resistant roots. Now they grow in dense thickets amid the dead tree trunks. Another pioneer plant is *Chenopodium graveolens*. (I've never found a common name for it; the scientific name translates as "strong-smelling goosefoot.") A few specimens still grow in disturbed areas. The plants are most notice-

able in autumn when they turn brilliant red. The stems are square in cross-section and the flowers are tiny, scabby-looking lumps in the angles of the branches. But smell a crushed leaf. The homely little plant then gives off a wonderful minty odor.

The tree stumps are riddled with woodpecker holes. After the fire, many kinds of woodpecker flew to the mesas to feed on tree-boring insects infesting the dead forest. Bird-watchers came from across the country to observe flocks of northern three-toed woodpeckers. (Most woodpeckers have four toes arranged in opposite pairs on each foot.) Northern three-toed woodpeckers ordinarily occur in isolated populations in the high mountains of the West and are not normally found in the monument. Much more common is the downy woodpecker, about five inches long with black barred wings, a white stripe down its back and, in the male, a distinctive red patch on the back of the head. The hairy

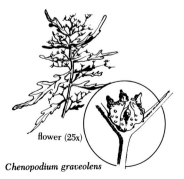

flower (25x)

Chenopodium graveolens

dh

bl

The "Y," 1976 (above) and 1981. The mesa between Frijoles and Alamo canyons suffered the most devastation from the fire.

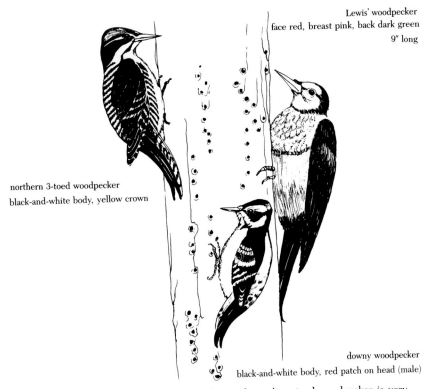

Lewis' woodpecker
face red, breast pink, back dark green
9" long

northern 3-toed woodpecker
black-and-white body, yellow crown

downy woodpecker
black-and-white body, red patch on head (male)

Some woodpeckers of the high desert. The northern three-toed woodpecker is very rare.

woodpecker is similar, but rarer and larger—about seven inches long. Flickers, also members of the woodpecker family, are numerous. They are easily identified by the salmon-colored flash of the undersides of their wings as they fly. In the autumn, Lewis' woodpeckers migrate into the monument area from the Rio Grande Valley. They are especially colorful, with red face and breast, white collar, and dark green back. All woodpeckers have stiff tails which they use to brace themselves as they drill with their stout bills into tree trunks. It is rare when the blackened forest does not ring with a

woodpecker's drumming.

The trail proceeds to the Y (actually, a delta in shape). From the Y the left-hand branch continues east, becoming the Frijoles Rim Trail; by this route it is 5.5 miles to the Visitor Center. The Upper Alamo Trail turns south (right) one mile to Alamo Canyon, which it enters by a gentle descent through a side canyon. Alamo Canyon escaped the fire and remains heavily forested. The climb out of Alamo to the south is gentle, relatively speaking, and offers views of the canyon which are as striking as those at the middle crossing or from the giant potreros near the canyon's mouth.

The mesas separating upper Alamo and Capulin canyons were once covered with black jack pines, but also were burned in La Mesa Fire. Signs of devastation and recovery are the same: broken tree trunks and carpets of slender wheatgrass. Deer and elk signs are abundant, especially in winter. Here again the trail divides. The right-hand branch continues south into Capulin Canyon, descending the 600-foot north wall by a series of switchbacks. From this trail the view of the San Miguel Mountains is splendid.

The second branch turns left, southeast toward Stone Lions. The ponderosa pine forest grades into pinyon-juniper; here the fire burned itself out. As it approaches Stone Lions the trail descends the Pajarito Fault. The tread is rough and rocky, but the view is one of the most striking in the monument. The barren potreros flanking Alamo Canyon stretch toward White Rock Canyon and the Cerros del Rio Plateau. The Rio Grande Valley, bounded on the east by the Sangre de Cristo Mountains, extends south beyond Albuquerque and north to Colorado.

Below the scarp the trail divides again. The right-hand branch turns south one mile to Capulin Canyon. The main trail proceeds east to the Stone Lions Shrine, less than a quarter-mile away. It is a six-mile return trip to the Visitor Center via the Stone Lions Trail.

flicker
white breast, brownish wings
salmon-colored underwings
11″ long

Trails originating at
ST. PETER'S DOME

Three trails, Capulin Canyon, Boundary Peak, and Picacho, originate near St. Peter's Dome, high point of the San Miguel Mountains. The Dome may be approached from State Road 4 at a junction eleven miles west of the monument entrance, where Dome Road, Forest Road 289, heads south (left) 6.5 miles to Forest Road 142. This 3.5-mile spur leads east (left) to the Forest Service lookout atop St. Peter's Dome.

An alternate route from the southern end of the monument begins at Cochiti Dam. Forest Road 268 leads through the community at Cochiti toward Cochiti Canyon and the San Miguel Mountains. It is paved as far as the Cochiti Lake golf course. About 4.5 miles west of the dam is the junction with Forest Road 289, which heads north (right) eight miles to the junction with Forest Road 142. From there it is 3.5 miles east (right) to the lookout.

These forest roads are unpaved and often in poor condition. They are, at best, only marginally suitable for passenger cars. After a series of hard rains, they can become nearly impassable.

The Capulin Canyon and Boundary Peak trails share a common trailhead where Forest Road 142 makes a sharp turn onto the east face of the San Miguel Mountains. The trailhead to the Picacho Trail is at the old picnic area below the Dome Lookout.

bl

Above the cliffs of upper Capulin Canyon rises Rabbit Hill, a volcanic vent cone.

CAPULIN CANYON

Beauty is in the eye of the beholder, and to many hikers, Capulin Canyon, with its level floor, sheltering pines and dancing stream, is the jewel of the monument. The upper part is choked with lush growth of the mixed-fir association, while Painted Cave at the lower end overlooks a broad and sandy wash bordered by stunted junipers.

Capulin Canyon is most easily reached from St. Peter's Dome in the San Miguel Mountains. The trail proceeds north from the trailhead, immediately beginning a long descent down a steep, wooded slope. The view to the north is of upper Capulin Canyon, Rabbit Hill, and the rim of the Jemez (Valles) Caldera. Within the canyon the trail to the Park Service cabin in middle Capulin is especially delightful. The bright green color of box-elders contrasts with cinnamon-colored bark of ponderosa pines, which grow especially large in this favored location. Watch for a "squirrel tree," one with fresh bundles of long ponderosa needles scattered beneath it. Tassel-eared (Abert's) squirrels feed on the cortical tissue of ponderosa twigs, biting through the stem and clipping off the terminal needle cluster. Not all trees are acceptable to the squirrels—only those especially low in certain organic compounds called monoterpenes, which are both bitter and mildly toxic. Squirrels can severely defoliate favored trees.

Despite the name, there are no capulins (chokecherries) in Capulin Canyon. The shrub growing

to Upper Alamo Trail

Forest Road 142

Boundary Peak Trail

St. Peter's Dome

to Turkey Spring

administrative cabin

to Stone Lions

Capulin Canyon

Painted Cave

Lower Alamo Trail

CAPULIN CANYON TRAIL

Administrative Cabin to:

St. Peter's Dome Road	3.5 mi	6.9 km	1900-ft ascent
Painted Cave	3.7	5.6	carry water

bl
Desert olive is the most common shrub in Capulin Canyon.

in thickets beside the stream is desert olive, a common plant in moist canyons of the Pajarito Plateau.

At the administrative cabin, a sign reads "Turkey Spring 4 miles." An arrow points west up the canyon wall. This is the junction with the Cañada-Capulin Trail. Downstream along the Capulin Trail, designated campgrounds line the stream for the next half mile between the cabin and the junction with the trail from Stone Lions. Heavy usage has made it necessary to regulate camping in Capulin Canyon; this is the only place in the wilderness where camping is controlled. From the Stone Lions Trail junction it is 2.5 miles farther south to Painted Cave.

Lower Capulin Canyon is broad and shallow. At Painted Cave it is nearly a half-mile wide but only 400 feet deep. When compared with the terrain upstream the country here is arid and barren; the little stream usually has disappeared into the sand before reaching Painted Cave. But here are ruins and the garden plots of the ancient inhabitants, together with one of the truly unique sights of the Southwest.

A broad, level floor with sheltering pines distinguishes upper Capulin Canyon. bl

84

Painted Cave, 50 feet above the canyon floor, is closed to visitors. The paintings are bl easily seen and photographed from below.

Not really a cave but rather an arched depression 30 feet up the cliff face, Painted Cave—La Cueva Pintada—was accessible for many years by means of a series of hand-and-toe holds. Bandelier himself described making the climb, commenting that he enlarged the cuts in the rock with his hammer. The cave is now closed to the public, but the paintings can be seen well enough from the ground.

Bandelier visited the cave twice in 1880. His descriptions are still appropriate: "It is a grand portal, of volcanic tuff; below are the signs of the cave-houses. . . . At a height of 10 meters are the paintings, red, in a semicircle. Hands and many with the cross. Juan José tells me that these were made by shepherds, who dwelt frequently in this cave." And later: "It is difficult to ascertain what is old and [what is]

not, as the cave has been the resort of shepherds so many, many years. Enormous blocks of rock have fallen right in front of the ruins of the cliff houses, and I suppose that this decay has taken place since the village was abandoned or that it was perhaps one of the causes of its destruction. . . ."*

The trail continues down the canyon a mile to the junction with Lower Alamo Trail, which snakes up and over the dark mesa separating the mouths of Alamo and Capulin Canyons. It is eleven miles to the Visitor Center by this route, which is the one followed by Adolph Bandelier on his first visit to Frijoles Canyon on October 23, 1880. Parts of this trail may be blocked by high waters of Cochiti Lake.

Lange and Riley, *The Southwestern Journals.* p. 172, 206–207

The Santo Domingo Basin of the Rio Grande Rift from the San Miguel Mountains. The Cerros del Rio volcanic field separates this basin from the Española Basin to the north.

BOUNDARY PEAK TRAIL

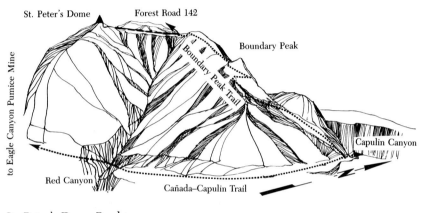

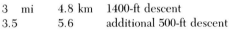

St. Peter's Dome Road to:			
Cañada-Capulin Trail	3 mi	4.8 km	1400-ft descent
Administrative Cabin	3.5	5.6	additional 500-ft descent

Boundary Peak Trail descends 1,400 feet down the east face of the San Miguel Mountains. It is a good trail with a gentle grade, but even were it not, the views make the trip worthwhile. To the southeast is the Santo Domingo Basin of the Rio Grande Rift, with Cochiti Lake a prominent feature. The Rio Grande flows toward Albuquerque at the foot of Sandia Mountain. Across the basin are the Ortiz and San Pedro Mountains, site of the Cerrillos Mining District, one of the oldest in the New

World. Thirteenth-century Indians dug turquoise there and exported it to Chaco Canyon, 150 miles to the west. The Old Placers were worked there for gold in the 1820s, and the New Placers in the 1840s. The coal-mining town of Madrid was established in the foothills in 1835.

North of the Ortiz Mountains, the Sangre de Cristo Range lines the eastern margin of the Rio Grande Rift. The Cerros del Rio volcanic field separates the Española and Santo Domingo Ba-

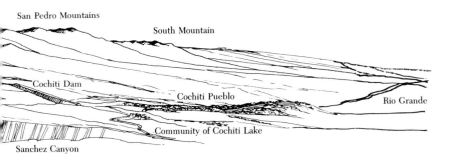

San Pedro Mountains

South Mountain

Cochiti Dam

Cochiti Pueblo

Rio Grande

Community of Cochiti Lake

Sanchez Canyon

sins. White Rock Canyon is visible as a jagged line dividing the orange potreros of the Pajarito Plateau from the black basalt of the Cerros del Rio. At the southern boundary of the Cerros del Rio Plateau is La Bajada Escarpment, which is clearly visible as it curves in a southeasterly direction from Cochiti Lake toward the Ortiz Mountains.

The common trailhead of the Boundary Peak and Capulin trails is at St. Peter's Dome. Where the Capulin Trail immediately turns north into Capulin Canyon, Boundary Peak Trail heads east, skirting the narrow ridge that extends toward the distinctive volcanic spire which lies about a half-mile from the road. The west boundary of the monument runs due north-south over the summit of Boundary Peak.

The trail continues around the south flank of Boundary Peak, through the Park Service fence and down a broad shoulder of the wooded slope. The trees are alligator junipers. The origin of the name is obvious; the bark is sectioned into squares like the hide of an alligator. Alligator juniper is more common and widespread in southern New Mexico and Arizona, where individual trees become massive. Trunks can grow to a diameter of three feet. Even here, at the northernmost limit of their range, some trees are impressive. The berries of this species are more palatable than those of other junipers, mealy and rather sweet, although the four little seeds are as hard as granite. Indians did not discriminate among juniper species. They ate the seeds and used the aromatic leaves medicinally and even mystically. Indeed, cultures

dh

Alligator juniper bark is unmistakable.

87

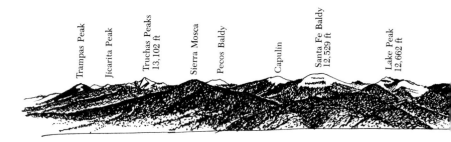

Trampas Peak
Jicarita Peak
Truchas Peaks 13,102 ft
Sierra Mosca
Pecos Baldy
Capulin
Santa Fe Baldy 12,529 ft
Lake Peak 12,662 ft

The Sangre de Cristo Mountains dominate the eastern horizon.

throughout the world attribute rejuvenating powers to the junipers. Even the name, from Latin *juvenis*, "youth," and *papere*, "producing," reflects this ancient belief.

As the trail continues its descent the forest changes to ponderosa pine on north-facing slopes, and then to pinyon-oneseed juniper on the slopes of tuff. Look for the lemonade bush, a large shrub that can grow six feet high. In spring, tiny yellow flowers bloom before the leaves come out. As the specific name implies, the leaves are divided into three lobes. In summer the plant bears tart, sticky red berries that make an acceptable lemonade. In autumn the leaves turn a brilliant red. The plant is related to poison ivy but is free of oily irritants. Indian women split the woody stems and wove the strips into baskets. The wood was

second only to that of willows for this use.

At the rim of Capulin Canyon, Boundary Peak Trail joins Cañada-Capulin Trail. This provides a good route from Painted Cave to the trailhead at St. Peter's Dome, being less steep than the Capulin Trail.

berries red-orange

lemonade bush, skunkbush
Rhus trilobata

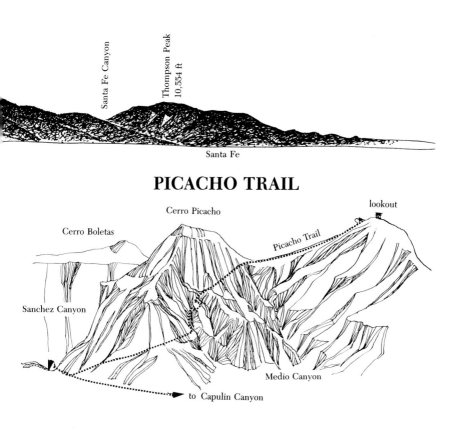

Santa Fe Canyon

Thompson Peak
10,554 ft

Santa Fe

PICACHO TRAIL

Cerro Picacho

Cerro Boletas

lookout

Picacho Trail

Sanchez Canyon

Medio Canyon

to Capulin Canyon

St. Peter's Dome Road to:				
Cañada-Capulin Trail	3	mi	4.8 km	steep 1500-ft descent
Eagle Canyon Pumice Mine	5		8	

The Picacho Trail lies entirely within the Santa Fe National Forest. It traverses a unit of the National Wilderness Preservation System contiguous with the Bandelier Wilderness. The area is open to hunting; the season for big game begins before the first of November. The trail links St. Peter's Dome with the Cañada-Capulin Trail near the north rim of Sanchez Canyon. Views from this trail are as fine as any in the monument.

The trail begins at the old picnic area near the Dome Lookout. Before starting the hike, it is well worth the time and effort to make the quarter-mile climb up to the lookout itself. As is traditional with lookouts, the view is fabulous. In addition to the sweeping panorama of the Rio Grande Rift to the south and east, an equally imposing scene opens to the north and west. The large mountain lying to the north is Redondo Peak, with Redondito on its flank. Both lie in

89

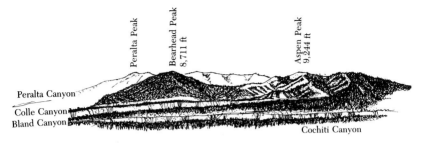

Peralta Peak

Bearhead Peak
8,711 ft

Aspen Peak
9,244 ft

Peralta Canyon

Colle Canyon

Bland Canyon

Cochiti Canyon

The southern skirt of the Jemez Volcanic Pile harbored a low-grade gold mining district at the turn of the century.

the center of the Jemez (Valles) Caldera. These two peaks are part of a large structure called a *resurgent dome*. They could be compared to a blister, with warping of overlying rocks by a shallow intrusion of molten rock for tens of thousands of years after the caldera collapse. Cerro Pelado, "bald hill," lies on the caldera's south rim. Aspen and Bearhead peaks mark a long ridge to the west. Below this ridge lie Bland and Colle Canyons, once centers of the Cochiti Gold Mining District. This low-grade gold and silver field experienced a mild boom and spectacular bust at the turn of the century. On the far horizon, 85 miles away, is Mount Taylor, a massive volcanic pile near Grants. It was named for Zachary Taylor, twelfth president of the United States.

Hikers pass under colorful standing rocks along the Picacho Trail.

bl

From the picnic area Picacho Trail skirts the Dome to the west, and then descends to the Picacho saddle a mile and one-half away. The rock here is not tuff but andesite. Andesite, the material of which the San Miguel Mountains are built, is a volcanic rock containing less silica than rhyolite but more than basalt. (The Bandelier tuff is compacted rhyolitic ash.) The San Miguels are outliers of the Paliza Canyon Formation, which is centered about ten miles to the west. They were formed some 10 million years before the Jemez ash flows.

Cerro Picacho, however, is a separate formation, younger than the San Miguel mass surrounding it, though by only a few million years. It is a volcanic vent which spewed forth thick, pasty rhyolitic lava. Several other peaks on the south slope of the caldera are similar to it. These include Rabbit Hill, as well as Aspen and Bearhead Peaks. The top of Cerro Picacho is a narrow wedge, rather like a screwdriver in shape. It is easily climbed through the pine forest on the northwest slope. The view from the top, especially into San-chez Canyon on Picacho's southwestern flank, is grand. *Picacho* translates as "peak," but has the connotation of a bump, like a mosquito bite. The name seems inappropriate as seen from this angle, but appears quite suitable when the peak is viewed edge-on, as it is from Interstate 25 near La Bajada Hill.

The trail crosses the north face of Cerro Picacho, passing through wonderfully contorted zones of rhyolitic rock. It descends through a group of standing rocks, the only incidence of these delightful formations in the area, and reaches the east slope of the cerro where an unobstructed view of Cochiti Dam and the Rio Grande opens up. The Picacho Trail joins the Cañada-Capulin Trail near the rim of Sanchez Canyon. It is a moderate two-mile hike west (right) through Sanchez Canyon to the Dome Road at the Eagle Canyon pumice mine. This option requires making car shuttle arrangements. An alternative route leads east (left) on the Cañada-Capulin Trail to the Boundary Peak Trail and back up to St. Peter's Dome, a distance of eight miles.

Trailhead at
EAGLE CANYON PUMICE MINE

The Cañada-Capulin Trail leads across Forest Service land and into the monument from the south. Trailhead is at the abandoned Eagle Canyon Pumice Mine on Forest Road 289 about four miles north of its junction with Forest Road 268 in Cochiti Canyon. This southern approach from Cochiti Dam is more suitable for passenger cars than the alternate 10.5 miles down Forest Road 289 (Dome Road) from State Road 4 in the Jemez Mountains. These unpaved forest roads are often in poor condition, especially after a series of rains.

The pumice mine is located at a sharp bend in Forest Road 289 just below a steep cliff into which the road has been cut. The trail is numbered Forest Trail 118.

CAÑADA-CAPULIN TRAIL

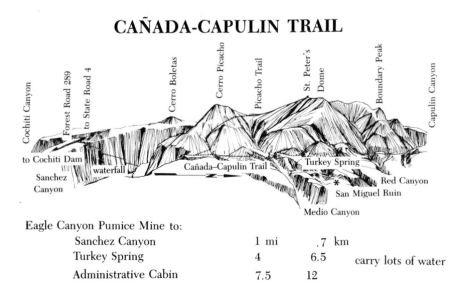

Eagle Canyon Pumice Mine to:

Sanchez Canyon	1 mi	.7 km
Turkey Spring	4	6.5 carry lots of water
Administrative Cabin	7.5	12

Cañada-Capulin Trail traverses lonely mesas south and west of Capulin Canyon. Much of the trail is on Forest Service land. This area, the Dome Wilderness, is open to hunting and is a traditional hunting ground of the Cochiti Indians. Water is available at three points: Sanchez Canyon, Turkey Spring and Capulin Canyon. This is unsafe to drink without treatment, as is all other open water on the Pajarito Plateau.

The trail begins at the southern end of the Dome Road at the old Eagle Canyon pumice mine, now inactive. The mine was an open pit; pumice was merely scooped out of the hillside. Pumice erupted from the Jemez volcano as airborne debris before the ash flows began. Deposits underlie the tuff formations of the Pajarito Plateau and are exposed at its perimeter. Pumice mines are still active elsewhere on the plateau. Pumice is a light, glassy lava so full of airholes that it floats on water. It is used in scouring powders and polishing preparations, and to make lightweight building blocks.

The name Eagle Canyon commemorates prospector Joseph Eagle, one of the developers of the Cochiti Gold Mining District. Activity was centered in Bland Canyon a few miles to the west. Speculators pumped millions of dollars into the mining of low-grade ore between 1890 and 1905, but realized little return on the investment. A 1967 report notes that the value of pumice taken from the Jemez Mountains had by that time surpassed the value of all the gold and silver recovered from the Cochiti Gold Mining District.

Nature has reclaimed the Eagle Canyon Pumice Mine. Spoil piles have been reduced to hillocks by erosion and are covered with rabbit brush. Small pines crowd the slopes and the old road has almost washed away.

The trail tops a gentle rise and begins descent into Sanchez Canyon, southernmost of the massive, straight-walled canyons that cut the Pajarito Plateau. A permanent stream courses through upper Sanchez; the trail crosses just above a fine 80-foot waterfall. The Cochiti Indians called this canyon *Tyesht-ye ka-ma chinaya*, "arroyo of the place of the waterfall." Early maps list it as Cañón José Sanchez after a settler who owned land there.

The trail through Sanchez Canyon is moderate, with a gentler grade than that through Frijoles or Alamo Canyons. The terrain is dry, with junipers dominating the landscape. Cerro Picacho sits on the north rim with a fine set of cliffs overlooking the trail. Just beyond the north edge of Sanchez Canyon is the junction with the Picacho Trail that climbs 1,500 feet up the steep slope to St. Peter's Dome. The Cañada-Capulin Trail continues north, passing through the dry, rough fingers of Medio Canyon at the base of the San Miguels.

Alligator junipers line the trail. On open slopes the dominant shrub is Apache plume, a member of the rose family. In spring and into summer it bears large white flowers resembling wild roses. The plant is especially striking after the seeds have set and their fluffy plumed tails shine and glow in the

flowers white

Apache plume

Fallugia paradoxa

afternoon sun. The wood of Apache plume is hard; Indians used it to make arrows.

The trail crosses the largest of the branches of Medio Canyon, in which a small spring usually feeds a puddle or two of water. Then it climbs the north slope and enters the monument. Off to the southeast is San Miguel ruin. No trail leads to the site, and even experienced hikers equipped with topographic maps have trouble locating it. It sits on a barren and exposed mesa overlooking Medio Canyon. San Miguel is not a large ruin, less than half the size of Yapashi. According to Keres tradition, San Miguel was the third settlement (the first two being Tyuonyi and Yapashi) occupied by the Cochiti during their migration from Frijoles Canyon to their present home on the Rio Grande.

bl

San Miguel Ruin appears better preserved than most ruins of the Pajarito Plateau. Potsherd dating indicates occupation periods contemporaneous with Yapashi and Tyuonyi.

Edgar Lee Hewett, in his turn-of-the-century studies, dated the ruin between 1250 and 1500, contemporaneous with the other two. No further study of San Miguel has been done.

Within a quarter-mile of the boundary fence, the trail crosses a small stream, the outflow of Turkey Spring. This and several smaller springs owe their existence to a bed of water-bearing sandstone that crops out on the east face of the San Miguel Mountains. It is a member of the Santa Fe group of sediments that fill the Rio Grande Rift.

I once saw a turkey in the monument, but not at Turkey Spring. Until the 1940s the birds were common on the Pajarito Plateau. Adolph Bandelier mentions them often in his journals, and homesteaders to the north considered them pests. A few turkeys still occur at higher elevations in the Jemez Mountains. The Park Service is identifying and further protecting their range within the monument.

North of Turkey Spring the trail passes out of the pumice and tuff of the Bandelier formation and into the red beds of the Galisteo Formation. Unlike the cliffs and mesas

turkey

surrounding it, the Galisteo is not volcanic in origin. It is made up of mudstones, sandstones and conglomerates that were laid down some 58 million years ago. The Galisteo predates and underlies the Santa Fe group and is exposed here along an ancient fault. At Red Canyon, two miles north of Turkey Spring, the trail passes out of the Galisteo red beds. Note that the cliffs downstream are again Bandelier tuff. The Galisteo Formation also is exposed along Interstate 25 on La Bajada hill south of Santa Fe.

The Keres called Capulin Canyon *Api'intsi'i;* Adolph Bandelier called it *Cañón de la Questa Colorada*. Both names mean "canyon of the red slope" and make reference to this red soil, though it is not exposed in Capulin Canyon itself. The present name comes from Capulin Mesa that separates Capulin and Red canyons. In the 1890s Americans living in Cochiti Canyon began using the name. Both "Capulin" and "Cañón de la Questa Colorada" were used loosely and interchangeably until the 1920s.

At the south rim of Capulin Canyon is the junction with the Boundary Peak Trail that climbs to St. Peter's Dome. Then the trail descends down a pleasant pine-covered slope into Capulin Canyon. Note white ceramic insulators on some trees. These are remains of a telephone line that once served the entire Pajarito Plateau. The line was a single bare wire, a so-called ground-return system. Service was interrupted during rainstorms when wet branches made contact with the

The contorted tuff canyons of the Pajarito Plateau make fine playgrounds for timid bl explorers. Pets are permitted on Forest Service land.

wire and shorted it out. The phone was a socializing and civilizing force in the lives of local homesteaders. Evelyn Frey tells of reading newspapers over the phone to lonely snowbound settlers she never met, and of conducting a romance between separated lovers by relaying messages over the telephone. The line was multiparty; a ring, actuated by a hand crank, was heard at every phone. Anyone could listen in. Three rings signaled an emergency. Several boxes containing telephones were placed in the monument for the safety and convenience of visitors. The line was abandoned during World War II.

The Cañada-Capulin trail terminates at the administrative cabin in Capulin Canyon where it ties into the trail network servicing the wilderness.

In 1889, Adolph Bandelier wrote in *The Delight Makers:* ". . . these bald-crested mountains, dark and forbidding as they appear from a distance, conceal and shelter in their deep gorges and clefts many a spot of great natural beauty, surprisingly picturesque, but difficult of access."*

They still do.

Adolph Bandelier with Juan Jose Montoya of Cochiti Pueblo at Painted Cave, December 1, 1880. Photo by George C. Bennett. *Archives, Maxwell Museum of Anthropology, University of New Mexico.*

Bandelier, *The Delight Makers.* p. 1

97

GLOSSARY

alamo   *Span.*   poplar, cottonwood

Albuquerque   Albuquerque, New Mexico was named for the Duke of Alburqu-
                 erque, Viceroy of Mexico in 1706, the year the settlement was founded.
                 (The first "r" in the name was subsequently dropped.) The word
                 itself means "white oak," from Latin *albus*, white, and *querqus*, oak.

andesite   *geol.*   a volcanic rock intermediate in silica content between basalt
                 and rhyolite. Named for the Andes mountains of South America.

ancho   *Span.*   broad, wide

bajada   *Span.*   descent, slope

basalt   *geol.*   a fine-grained, heavy, crystalline volcanic rock dark in color
                 and rich in iron and magnesium compounds; poorest of all volcanic
                 rock in silica. Pronounced buh-salt'.

blanca   *Span.*   white

boleta   *Span.*   admission ticket, ballot

bolita   *Span.*   little ball

burro   *Span.*   donkey

caldera   A large crater formed by volcanic explosion or by collapse of a vol-
                 canic cone. From Latin *caldaria*, cauldron.

cañada   *Span.*   ravine, gully

capulin   *Span.*   chokecherry (*Prunus virginiana*)

CCC   Civilian Conservation Corps, a Federal program established in 1933
                 to provide jobs for unemployed single young men during the Great
                 Depression. Abolished in 1942.

cerro   *Span.*   hill

chapero   *Span.*   "It is said that the name means in New Mexico Spanish
                 'abrupt point of a mesa,' also 'old slouch hat.' " [Harrington (1916),
                 p. 414.] The word is not known in present-day New Mexico.

cholla   *colloq. Span.*   skull, head

colorado   *Span.*   red, ruddy

98

dacite	*geol.*	a volcanic rock intermediate in silica content between andesite and rhyolite. Named for the Roman province Dacia, present-day Rumania.
dioecious	*bot.*	having male and female flowers on separate plants, from Greek *di*, two, and *oikos*, house.
encina	*Span.*	evergreen oak
española	*Span.*	Spanish woman
family	*bot.*	a group of plants of similar flower structure. Members of a family are further classified as to genus and species.
feral		wild animals descended from domesticated ancestors
frijoles	*Span.*	beans
frijolito	*Span.*	little bean
grande	*Span.*	large, great, grand
Ha'atse	*Keres*	earth, world
hondo	*Span.*	deep
Jemez		from the Towa word *hemish*, people, used by the Jemez Indians in reference to themselves. Towa is the Jemez language.
kiva	*Hopi*	a ceremonial chamber
lava	*geol.*	molten rock released at the earth's surface during a volcanic eruption. Also, the same material cooled and hardened. From Latin *lavare*, to wash.
magma	*geol.*	molten rock confined beneath the surface of the earth. It becomes lava if it breaks through to the surface. From Greek *massein*, kneaded.
medio	*Span.*	middle
midden		a refuse heap, particularly of a primitive habitation.
montoso	*Span.*	heavily wooded. Montoso Peak has only scraggly pinyon-juniper thickets.
norte	*Span.*	north
pajarito	*Span.*	little bird
pelado	*Span.*	bald

peña	*Span.* rock
petroglyph	a drawing scratched on rock. From Greek *petros*, stone, and *glyphe*, carving.
picacho	*Span.* peak, summit
potrero	*Span.* pastureland. Bandelier applied the term to the tongue-like mesas of the Pajarito Plateau. He seems to have thought that the word implies a pillar or gigantic post. [Bandelier (1892), p. 158.]
questa	*Span.* slope
redondo	*Span.* round
rio	*Span.* river
rito	*Span.* creek (i.e., little river)
rhyolite	*geol.* a volcanic rock high in free silica, frequently light in color and having a texture that shows flow patterns. From the Greek *rhyax*, stream, and *lithos*, stone
sandia	*Span.* watermelon
sangre	*Span.* blood
sepal	*bot.* one of the parts of the outer covering of a flower, enclosing the petals.
vaca	*Span.* cow. Lange (1966) suggests (p. 225) that Bandelier erred in naming the mesa "Potrero de las Vacas," and that a Keres term, *wákós*, ladder, was more appropriate.
valle	*Span.* valley

SELECTED REFERENCES

Aubele, Jayne C. 1976. Geology of the Cerros del Rio Volcanic Field, New Mexico M.S. Thesis. Albuquerque: University of New Mexico.

Bandelier, Adolph F. 1946. *The Delight Makers*. New York: Dodd, Mead & Co.

————. 1976. *Final Report of Investigations among the Indians of the Southwestern United States Carried on Mainly in the Years from 1880 to 1885. Part II*. Papers of the Archaeological Institute of America. American Series. IV. New York: AMS Press, Inc. Originally published by the Cambridge University Press, 1890–1892.

Bousman, C. Britt. 1974. *Archaeological Assessment at Bandelier National Monument*. Dallas: Southern Methodist University.

Chapin, Charles E. 1979. "Evolution of the Rio Grande Rift—A Summary." In *Rio Grande Rift: Tectonics and Magmatism*, edited by Robert E. Riecker. Washington, D.C.: American Geophysical Union.

Chapman, Richard C., and Biella, Jan V. 1980. "4,000 Years on the Southern Pajarito Plateau." *Exploration, Annual Bulletin of the School of American Research:* 7–10. Santa Fe: School of American Research.

Fiske, Turbesé Lummis, and Lummis, Keith. 1975. *Charles F. Lummis: the Man and His West*. Norman: University of Oklahoma Press.

Foxx, Teralene S., and Potter, Loren D. 1978. *Fire Ecology at Bandelier National Monument. Final Report*. Santa Fe: National Park Service.

Griggs, Roy L. 1964. *Geology and Ground-Water Resources of the Los Alamos Area New Mexico*. Washington, D.C.: Geological Survey Water-Supply Paper 1753.

Harrington, John Peabody. 1916. *The Ethnogeography of the Tewa Indians*, 29th Annual Report, 1907–1908, Bureau of American Ethnology, Smithsonian Institute. Washington, D.C.: Government Printing Office.

Hendron, Jerome W. 1946. *Frijoles: A Hidden Valley in the New World*. Santa Fe: Rydal Press, Inc.

Lange, Charles H., and Riley, Carroll L. 1966. *The Southwestern Journals of Adolph F. Bandelier 1880–1882*. Albuquerque: University of New Mexico Press.

Martin, William C., and Hutchins, Charles R. 1981. *A Flora of New Mexico* (in 2 volumes). Vaduz, Liechtenstein: A. R. Gantner Verlag K.G.

Smith, R. L.; Bailey, R. A.; and Ross, C. S. 1970. Geologic Map of the Jemez Mountains, New Mexico. Washington, D.C.: U.S. Geological Survey.

Steen, Charlie R. 1977. Pajarito Plateau Archaeological Survey and Excavations. Los Alamos: Los Alamos Scientific Laboratory Report LASL-77-4.

ANIMALS

bear, 72
chipmunk, 22
deer, 41
elk, 40
exclosure, 71
salamander, 45
sheep, 35, 42, 56
squirrel, 22, 83

BIRDS

bluebird, 72
crane, sandhill, 55
dipper, 23
flicker, 80
nighthawk, 37
raven, 61
swallow, violet-green, 37, 62
swift, white-throated, 61
turkey, 23, 95
vulture, 61
wren, canyon, 32
woodpeckers, 78

GEOLOGY

andesite, 17, 91, 98
ash, volcanic, 7, 32
basalt, 7, 98
caldera, 8, 98
Cerros del Rio, 8, 15, 17
Galisteo red beds, 95
Jemez Mountains, 8
maar, 16
Pajarito Plateau, vi, 7, 16, 93
pumice, 93
Rio Grande Rift, 7, 55, 95
Sandia Mountain, 55
San Miguel Mountains, 37, 91, 95
tent rocks, 15
tuff, 7, 15, 32, 66
White Rock Canyon, 8, 17, 59

INDIAN

cave dwellings, 13
farming, 35, 38, 48, 59, 62, 84
Keres, 3, 13, 70, 94
kiva, 13, 23, 48, 58, 99
occupation, vi, 3, 38, 48, 57
petroglyphs, 47, 100
pottery, 49, 57
shrines, 35, 69, 81
Tewa, 3, 13, 47, 70
use of animals, 22, 56
use of plants, 18, 20, 30, 33, 34, 40, 64, 76, 88, 94

PEOPLE

Abbott, Judge Judson, 5, 23, 29, 37
Bandelier, Adolph F., 1, 5, 16, 52, 54, 56, 59, 71, 73, 85, 95, 100
Blumenthal, Vera von, 49
Dugan, Rose, 49
Frey, Evelyn, 5, 6, 37, 97
Hewett, Edgar L., 5, 13, 23, 49, 53, 66, 95
Lummis, Charles F., 2, 54

PLACE NAMES

Alamo Canyon, 57, 64, 71, 80
Apache Spring, 42
Boundary Peak, 37, 87
Capulin Canyon, 83, 95
Ceremonial Cave, 22, 62
Cerrillos Mining District, 86
Cerros del Rio, 37, 55, 59, 71, 86
chapero, 56, 59, 73, 98
Cochiti Gold Mining District, 90, 93
Cochiti Lake, 20, 56, 73, 86
Corral Hill, 60, 63
Frijoles Rim Trail, 62, 80
Frijolito Ruin, 53
Jemez (Valles) Caldera, 52, 55, 83, 90
Jemez Mountains, 42, 56, 93
Kiva House, 58, 73
Lower Falls, 20
Lummis Canyon, 56, 64
Painted Cave, 84, 88
Pajarito Fault, 55, 70, 81
Pajarito Plateau, vi, 5, 7, 16, 35, 47, 71
Ponderosa Campground, 22, 28, 74
Rabbit Hill, 55, 83, 91
Red Canyon, 95
Rio Grande, 17, 20, 56, 73, 86
Rio Grande Valley, 80, 86
Rito de los Frijoles, 16, 20, 37, 74
Rocky Mountains, 55
Sanchez Canyon, 91, 93
Sandia Mountain, 55, 86, 100
Sangre de Cristo Mountains, 55
San Miguel Mountains, 37, 86, 91
San Miguel Ruin, 94
Santo Domingo Basin, 8, 86
Shrine of the Stone Lions, 69, 81
St. Peter's Dome, 37, 82
Turkey Spring, 95
Tyuonyi, 13, 32, 37, 52
Upper Crossing, 22, 26, 28, 45, 74
Upper Falls, 16
Visitor Center, 12, 51
White Rock Canyon, 20, 32, 56, 73, 87
"Y," 62, 80
Yapashi, 68

PLANTS

Apache plume, 93
aspen, 42, 44
bluestem, 39, 65, 72
box-elder, 18
buckbrush, 77
capulin, 19, 83, 98
Chenopodium graveolens, 78
chokecherry, 19, 83, 98
columbine, 26
cottonwood, 17
currant, 61
desert olive, 19, 84
dioecism, 18, 99
dropseed, 40
Douglas fir, 33, 43, 75
estafiata, 20
four o'clock, 55
Gambel oak, 19, 78
grama, 30
greenthread, 40
groundsel, 35
hop tree, 61
horsetail, 25
Indian paintbrush, 40
juniper, 30, 53, 87
lemonade bush, 88
lily, 43
locust, 61
lupine, 40
meadow rue, 26
mock-orange, 61
Mormon tea, 19

mountain mahogany, 34
mountain muhly, 40, 63
mountain spray, 61
mullein, 28, 65
nettle, 25, 45
onion, 77
pinyon, 29
poison ivy, 25, 45
ponderosa pine, 33, 39, 63, 83
sagebrush, 20
snakeweed, 35
tarragon, 35
three-awn, 40
valerian, 26
wheatgrass, 39, 77
white fir, 76
wormwood, 20
yucca, 34

GENERAL

CCC, 5, 13, 29, 42, 98
cross-country skiing, 38, 42
Forest Service, U.S., 5, 29, 37, 39, 49,
    82, 89, 92
hunting, 89, 93
La Mesa Fire, 38, 42, 76, 81
National Park Service, U.S., 5, 32, 39,
    42, 45, 54, 56, 72, 95
National Wilderness Preservation
    System, vii, 6, 89, 93
Rito de los Frijoles Grant, 4
safety, iv, 9
telephone, 95